# Breakthrough
# Windows Vista™
Find Your Favorite Features and
Discover the Possibilities

*Joli Ballew*
*S. E. Slack*

PUBLISHED BY

Microsoft Press
A Division of Microsoft Corporation
One Microsoft Way
Redmond, Washington 98052-6399

Library of Congress Control Number: 2006940674

Printed and bound in the United States of America.

1 2 3 4 5 6 7 8 9   QWT   2 1 0 9 8 7

Distributed in Canada by H.B. Fenn and Company Ltd.

A CIP catalogue record for this book is available from the British Library.

Microsoft Press books are available through booksellers and distributors worldwide. For further information about international editions, contact your local Microsoft Corporation office or contact Microsoft Press International directly at fax (425) 936-7329. Visit our Web site at www.microsoft.com/mspress. Send comments to mspinput@microsoft.com.

Microsoft, Microsoft Press, ActiveX, Aero, DirectX, Excel, Hotmail, Internet Explorer, MSN, OneCare, Outlook, PowerPoint, Windows, Windows CardSpace, Windows Live, Windows Media, Windows Vista, Xbox, Xbox 360, and Xbox Live are either registered trademarks or trademarks of Microsoft Corporation in the United States and/or other countries. Other product and company names mentioned herein may be the trademarks of their respective owners.

The example companies, organizations, products, domain names, e-mail addresses, logos, people, places, and events depicted herein are fictitious. No association with any real company, organization, product, domain name, e-mail address, logo, person, place, or event is intended or should be inferred.

This book expresses the author's views and opinions. The information contained in this book is provided without any express, statutory, or implied warranties. Neither the authors, Microsoft Corporation, nor its resellers, or distributors will be held liable for any damages caused or alleged to be caused either directly or indirectly by this book.

**Acquisitions Editor:** Juliana Aldous Atkinson
**Developmental Editor:** Sandra Haynes
**Project Editor:** Rosemary Caperton
**Editorial Production Services:** Happenstance Type-O-Rama

Body Part No. X13-24175

# CONTENTS AT A GLANCE

# CONTENTS

**What do you think of this book? We want to hear from you!**

Microsoft is interested in hearing your feedback so we can continually improve our books and learning resources for you. To participate in a brief online survey, please visit:

**www.microsoft.com/learning/booksurvey/**

**What do you think of this book? We want to hear from you!**

Microsoft is interested in hearing your feedback so we can continually improve our books and learning resources for you. To participate in a brief online survey, please visit:

**www.microsoft.com/learning/booksurvey/**

# Acknowledgments

Quite a few people made this book a success, and it took a team to bring it all together. It was a fun and inspiring book to write, and there are many people I want to thank for being a part of it. First, Sally Slack was once again a wonderful coauthor and a pleasure to work with. I would be honored to work with her again; however, I do worry a little about that odd sense of humor!

Next, I'd like to thank Laurie Stewart for her attention to detail, as well as all the people who worked tirelessly in the background: Sandra Haynes, developmental editor, and Rosemary Caperton, project editor (both from Microsoft Press); Kim Wimpsett, copy editor; Curt Simmons, technical reviewer; Chris Gillespie, designer and compositor; and Juliana Aldous Atkinson, who selected Sally and me to write this wonderful book in the first place.

Of course, I want to thank everyone at Studio B: my agent, Neil Salkind, who is always available and supportive; Lisa Pere, who keeps me in Microsoft articles and Webcasts; and Linda Thornton, who makes sure I'm always paid. Studio B has been a great asset this last half decade, and we make a good all-around team.

Finally, a special thanks to my family—Mom, Dad, Jennifer, and Cosmo—as well as Mindy, Bryan, Pam, Kim, Michelle, Brad, and all of my buddies at the local hangout for keeping me sane when I'm working too hard or not enough. It's always nice to find someone to IM (or hang out with) when I'm working and need a break!

—Joli Ballew


When I begin writing a book, I am never quite sure what's really going to come out of my brain. Thankfully, Joli Ballew knows how to keep me in check while letting the fun still flow. You are a joy to work with, girlfriend! Thank you for including me on this book; I sense a long and crazy collaborative future ahead for us.

A very special thank you to Neil Salkind, who continues to toil for me in the unrewarding background. I am so grateful to count you as a friend too. And to the women of Studio B—Linda, Renee, Lisa, Julie, Pam, and Lynn—thank you for answering my endless questions and keeping me in line.

As for Juliana, Sandra, and Rosemary at Microsoft: You ladies are a lovely team to work with. Your openness to new ideas and directions is a breath of fresh air! And I can't leave out a critical member of the team: Laurie Stewart is a woman of extreme patience, and, thankfully, organization is her middle name. This book wouldn't have made it to press on time without her. I echo Joli's thanks to those who worked silently in the background to make this book look cool, sound good, and be as accurate as possible.

My special thanks and love go to Greg and Alia, as always, and also to my brothers and dear sister who are always there when I need them. And boy, did I need you this year! Last but never least: Thanks, Mom and Dad, for encouraging me to work hard and follow my passion.

—Sally Slack

# Introduction

*Breakthrough Windows Vista.* This book is guaranteed to spark your imagination and change the way you work and play with your PC. The Windows Vista operating system will change the way you look at everything from digital photography to movie making to how you listen to music. Windows Vista will also change how you watch TV; view DVDs; and obtain, record, and manage any kind of media or data. Throw in a little instant messaging, some Web surfing, and a new e-mail program with junk mail filtering, and you're set for a long, long time! With Windows Vista, you can indeed *Breakthrough*!

While reading this book, let your imagination run wild. Although we'll introduce everything that's new in Windows Vista, including instant searching from the Start menu, using search folders, using the new Windows Sidebar and gadgets, and working with new programs such as Windows Photo Gallery, Media Player 11, and

*The Windows Vista operating system will change the way you look at everything....*

an improved Media Center, you can do much more with these new features than just what we'll offer here. That being said, although we will detail how to make a movie; how to watch, play, record, subscribe to, and manage all types of media; and how to sync a digital music player, we'll also offer jumping-off points to other projects, such as how to add a media extender and stream media throughout your home or how to get more from the available applications in Windows Vista.

Beyond the media aspect, though, Windows Vista also offers a built-in file system that lets you manage all your data more efficiently. Making sure you understand this file system is one of our top priorities, because if you can get started on the right foot and save data to the correct folders, create your own subfolders, and create a working file and folder system, you'll be much happier with your PC than you would if you continued to save data haphazardly to your hard drive. There's a lot more to it these days than just becoming proficient in the latest technologies and applications—today, you will use these technologies to enhance and improve your office, your home, and your life.

## What's in Store

This book is divided into six parts: "Getting Started," "Pictures," "Music," "Video," "Media Center," and "Everyday Living." Within the parts are chapters that contain all the information you need to get started with digital photographs, music, video, Media Center, and more.

In Part I, "Getting Started," you'll learn about what's new in Windows Vista and how to perform basic tasks you'll want to do immediately, such as connecting to the Internet and adding a new user account. Of course, getting started also includes personalizing your PC with screen savers and desktop backgrounds, enabling the Sidebar, optimizing the display, and getting to know the new file and folder structure, so we'll include all of that too.

In Part II, "Pictures," you'll learn how to create the ultimate photo library, how to perform basic tasks with Windows Photo Gallery, and what your options are for sharing your digital masterpieces. As noted, there will also be some jumping-off points; one of interest here is how to create a video blog!

In Part III, "Music," you'll learn how to listen to, share, manage, and optimize your listening experience for all things musical. With your home optimized for music, you'll then learn how to get more out of Media Player 11 by subscribing to online media, syncing mobile devices, and streaming music throughout your home.

In Part IV, "Video," you'll become skilled in working with video by fine-tuning your video library, importing video and making a quick movie, and jumping off into two video projects on your own.

Part V, "Media Center," brings it all together by showing you how Media Center works with other Windows Vista programs, from organizing and accessing your media to working with media extenders to recording your favorite television shows.

Finally, in Part VI, "Everyday Living," you'll see how Windows Vista can impact your everyday life through the use of features such as parental controls, games, Web browsing, e-mail, and more. Plus, you can jump off into creating coloring books, calendars, and more by incorporating the 2007 Microsoft Office system with Windows Vista.

# Special Elements in the Book

As you work through the book, you'll run across the following special elements that will help you get the most out of Windows Vista:

**Tips and notes**   Sound advice for getting better performance, better results, and whatever extra can be pulled from a given application or task. These suggestions offer guidance for performing tasks more effectively.

**Sidebars**   Stand-alone sections within the main body of a chapter. The sidebars are related to the chapter's topic but are completely independent of the chapter discussion. They offer ways to take your experiences even further. For instance, in Chapter 4, "Share Your Photos," a sidebar details how to compress a group of images prior to e-mailing them. Although this does relate to sharing photos, the sidebar takes the topic a bit further by expanding on sharing and e-mailing options.

**Clock**   An icon next to some sections that tells how much time a given task will take. This offers you a guide on how much time you should set aside for particular projects.

# **Getting** Ready

Before you get started, you should get your computer ready for the incredible tasks you're about to perform. If you have Windows Vista installed on your computer already, you're almost there. If not, no worries; the installation CD or DVD makes it easy to install the operating system as well as transfer data from an old computer to your new one. For more information about transferring data prior to an installation, see Chapter 2, "Set Up Windows Vista, and Create an Organizational System." Once installed (or before going any further), make sure to check for updates using Windows Update.

With Windows Vista installed and updated, continue getting ready by installing all of the media hardware you own one item at a time. This includes but is not limited to digital cameras, scanners, TV tuners, DVD recorders, DVD players, speakers, printers, headphones, portable music players, secondary monitors, external hard drives, network drives, and so on. Make sure to install them one item at a time, because if you don't have the proper hardware drivers, Windows Vista will automatically go online to try to find them. And chances are good that they'll install automatically, without any intervention from you. However, on the slim chance something doesn't install, you'll know exactly what it is, what it's called, and what parts did install and what didn't. (This is especially prevalent in TV tuners, where there are several items to install from the one device.) Take your time, and make sure everything is installed properly.

You may also want to check your system against the requirements listed on the Windows Vista minimum requirements list for the edition you selected. Say, for instance, that you have Windows Vista Ultimate, and you want to watch and record live TV. You must have a TV tuner installed to do that. If your system didn't come with one, well, you're not going to be able to watch and record live TV! You can get system information from the Welcome Center, as detailed in Chapter 1, "Take a Quick Tour."

# Support

We have made every effort to ensure the accuracy of this book. Microsoft Press provides corrections for books at *www.microsoft.com/mspress/support/search.asp*.

If you have comments, questions, or ideas regarding this book, please send them to Microsoft Press via e-mail (*mspinput@microsoft.com*).

For support for Windows Vista, you can connect to the Windows Vista Solution Center or the Microsoft Knowledge Base at *support.microsoft.com*. In the United States, Microsoft software product support issues not covered by the Microsoft Knowledge Base are addressed by Microsoft Product Support Services.

# PART I Getting Started

- **Explore the Welcome Center**
- **Explore the Start menu and instant search**
- **Search folders**
- **Personalize Windows Vista**
- **Use the Sidebar and gadgets**

# **Take** a Quick Tour

# CHAPTER 1

Congratulations on your new (or updated) PC with the Windows Vista operating system! Prepare to be blown away by the new features in Windows Vista and all the ways you can now incorporate your PC into your life and home. You're going to be astonished at how easy Windows Vista is to use. That's what this book is about—showing you how uncomplicated Windows Vista is, getting you going, starting you off on new ventures, and maybe even spurring a new hobby or two.

Because we want you to be as happy with your PC as possible, we'll start with a couple of chapters that will help you acquaint yourself with Windows Vista. In this first chapter, we'll introduce the basics, such as how the new Windows Vista features work and how to access them, and get you used to the

*Prepare to be blown away by the new features in Windows Vista and all the ways you can now incorporate your PC into your life and home.*

fact that Windows Vista performs a little differently and offers much more than earlier Windows versions. In the second chapter, we'll help you learn how folders are organized in Windows Vista and what you can do with them to keep your own data in check.

Once you're off and running, the remaining chapters will offer projects, broken down into small steps, that will help you do everything from organizing your picture library to using your PC as a media center. And we'll include a timeline too, so you know just what you're getting yourself into with each task. Don't worry, it'll be effortless. And fun!

# A Big Welcome from the Welcome Center

The first time you start Windows Vista, you'll get a nice, warm welcome from the Welcome Center. The Welcome Center offers a place to accomplish the tasks you'll want to perform right away, such as transferring files and settings from another computer, adding new users, connecting to the Internet, registering Windows, and personalizing Windows Vista. You can also use the Welcome Center to download and install, or sign up for, additional components such as Windows Live Toolbar, Windows Live OneCare, Windows Live Mail Desktop, and Windows Live Messenger. Figure 1-1 shows the Welcome Center.

### NAVIGATE THE WELCOME CENTER

Explore the Welcome Center to get a feel for what's available in it. What's New In Windows Vista will prove extremely helpful. Stay away from Transfer Files And Settings for now, though; we'll cover that in depth in Chapter 2.

To navigate the Welcome Center, follow these steps:

1. If the Welcome Screen is not open, click Start, and click Welcome Center to open it.

2. Under Get Started With Windows, click Show All 14 Items.

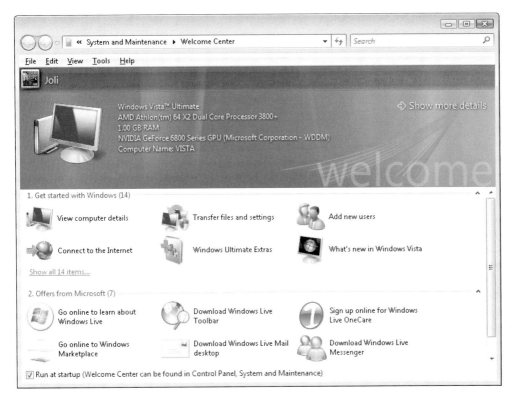

Figure 1-1: The Welcome Center offers a comprehensive place to get started with Windows Vista, including connecting to the Internet, adding new users, and accessing additional services and features.

❸ Click View Computer Details. Note the information at the top of the Welcome Center; it offers a brief description of Computer Details.

❹ Double-click View Computer Details to open System. System offers information including the Windows edition, system information, computer name, domain and workgroup settings, and the Windows activation status.

❺ Click the Back button to return to the Welcome Center, or if System opened in a new window, close that window to return.

❻ Click Add New Users. Note the information at the top of the Welcome Center; if offers a brief description of adding new users.

❼ Double-click Add New Users to open User Accounts And Family Safety. Again, click Back, or close the open window to return to the Welcome Center.

❽ Continue in this manner until you feel comfortable with the Welcome Center, and then close the Welcome Center.

## ADD A NEW USER

If you have more than one person in your home who will use the Windows Vista–based PC, you should create a user account for each of them. It's simple to do; just type the user name and configure a few settings, and you're off. Giving each person a user name (and password they control) will let them keep their data private from others who use the computer, will let them have their own settings for Windows Mail and Windows Internet Explorer, and more.

To create a new user account, follow these steps:

**1** In the Welcome Center, double-click Add New Users. You can also perform this task by using the User Accounts And Family Safety item in Control Panel, shown in Figure 1-2.

**2** Under User Accounts, click Add Or Remove User Accounts.

**3** Click Create A New Account.

**4** Type the new account name, and select Standard User or Administrator.

> **Standard User**   Select Standard User for most new users. This account type lets the user access most software and change system settings that do not affect other users or the security of the computer.

> **Administrator**   Select Administrator for those users who need complete access to the computer. Keep administrators to a minimum. This account type offers the user complete access; an administrator can make changes to the computer that affect every user, that affect system security, and that affect stability.

**5** Click Create Account.

**Figure 1-2:** Add user accounts from the Welcome Center or by using the User Accounts And Family Safety item in Control Panel.

You can manage the new account at any time. The best time is right after creating it. Click the new account to make changes to it, including creating a password, changing the picture, setting up parental controls, and changing the account name. (If desired, return to the Welcome Center.)

## CONNECT TO THE INTERNET

Connecting to the Internet from a new PC used to be painful. First, you had to find out where the settings were, and then, you had to work through a cryptic set of dialog boxes to configure the connection. Not anymore. You'll find an icon for connecting to the Internet right in the Welcome Center, making it simpler than ever to get online.

To connect to the Internet, follow these steps:

1. In the Welcome Center, double-click Connect To The Internet.

2. Select Set Up A New Connection.

3. Select Wireless, Broadband, or Dial-Up.

4. For Wireless, select the wireless network to use, and click Connect. For Broadband, type your user name, password, and connection name, and then click Connect. For Dial-Up, type the phone number to dial, user name, password, and connection name. Click Connect. For each, select Allow Other People To Use This Connection if you have others on your network who will also use this connection to access the Internet.

5. Click Close.

> **TROUBLESHOOTING** If you can't connect to the Internet, try resetting any routers, cable modems, or receivers, and try testing phone outlets as applicable. Your best bet for broadband is to turn everything off, including the PC; restart the cable modem and wait for it to initialize; restart the router and wait for it to initialize; and then restart the PC. Additionally, verify that any dial-up settings are correct, verify that the telephone outlet is functional, and verify all user names and passwords (they're often case-sensitive).

## REGISTER WINDOWS ONLINE

Registration is not mandatory like activation is; however, by registering, you'll get a lot of cool perks. You can sign up for e-mail that alerts you to upgrades, security alerts, new features and products, and more.

To register Windows Vista, follow these steps:

1. In the Welcome Center, double-click Register Windows Online.

2. On the Windows Vista Web site, click Continue Registration.

3. If you have a .NET or Microsoft Passport, a Hotmail address, an MSN e-mail address, or a Windows Live ID, type it along with your password. If you do not, follow the instructions to sign up for one.

4. You'll need to type information such as your e-mail address, name, and country. And, Microsoft will collect some information about your system, such as the product name, version, and type of computer hardware. Micro-soft will not share your information with anyone without your permission.

## DOWNLOAD AND INSTALL WINDOWS LIVE MESSENGER

Windows Live Messenger is an awesome instant messaging program. With it, you can set up video and voice conferences with anyone who has compatible software. You can send files, even really big ones you wouldn't dare send in an e-mail, play games with others, share files, give and receive remote assistance, and more.

Since Windows Live Messenger doesn't come with Windows Vista, you'll need to download and install it. If you've never downloaded and installed anything, you'll be happy to find that it's quite effortless.

To download and install Windows Live Messenger, follow these steps:

1. In the Welcome Center, under Offers From Microsoft, double-click Down-load Windows Live Messenger.

2. Read the information on the Windows Live Messenger home page, and click Get It Free.

3. In the File Download box, click Run.

4. When the download is complete, click Run.

5. When prompted to install Windows Live Messenger, click Next.

6. Read and accept the terms of the license agreement, and click Next.

⑦ Select the additional features you want. Click Next.

⑧ Click Continue to let the installation proceed.

⑨ When installation is complete, click Close.

⑩ Type your e-mail address and password to sign in. The e-mail address you'll use must be a .NET or Microsoft Passport, a Hotmail e-mail address, an MSN e-mail address, or a Windows Live ID.

> **TIP** If you're not yet familiar with Windows Live Messenger, sign in, and then refer to the Help options in the Windows Live Messenger interface.

# SIGN UP FOR FREE SERVICES

Options in the Welcome Center go far beyond getting started and downloading applications, as if those weren't enough! You can also sign up for the latest features. Two of our favorites are Windows Live OneCare and Windows Live Mail Desktop. To see all the offers, in the Welcome Center, under Offers From Microsoft, click Show All 7 Items.

## WINDOWS LIVE ONECARE

Windows Live OneCare offers round-the-clock protection and maintenance, including virus scanning, firewalls, tune-ups, file backups, and more. It's billed as a comprehensive PC care service, used to protect your computer from security threats, data loss, malware, spyware, and similar Internet threats. It's about $50 US per year for up to three computers.

## WINDOWS LIVE MAIL DESKTOP

This free feature helps you manage your e-mail accounts. These days, most people have at least two, generally one for work and one for play, and sometimes a third for online purchases or for logging on to Web sites notorious for selling e-mail addresses to spammers. You can use Windows Live Mail Desktop on your Windows Vista–based PC to organize your messages, your RSS feeds, and all your addresses, whether they are Web-based or not.

# The Start **Menu and Instant Search**

The new Start menu in Windows Vista looks and acts a little differently than the Start menu in earlier Microsoft operating systems. Sure, you still have immediate access to your documents, pictures, music, network, and Control Panel, but you'll see a few new items listed too. The new Start menu contains a link to your very own personal folder with your name on it and another for quick access to games.

What's really special is the new way to access programs, accessories, and system tools. Although you still have the ability to navigate through Start, All Programs to find the program you want, with Windows Vista you have a faster way to do this. Just type what you want to find in the Start Search box, and watch it magically appear in the Start menu's Programs list! This is called performing an *instant search*, and you'll learn how to do it next.

## PERFORM AN INSTANT SEARCH

Instant searches are amazing. No more browsing through folders and menus to find Paint. No more "exploring" the hard drive for a project you know the name of but aren't sure where it is. Instant searches will forever change the way you locate data on your PC.

To perform an instant search, follow these steps:

1. Click the Start button. It's the round, blue button at the bottom left of the desktop.

2. In the Start Search box, shown in Figure 1-3, type **paint**. Do *not* press Enter.

3. Look at the entries under Programs. Click Paint to open the application.

4. Click Start again.

5. Type your first name. Do *not* press Enter.

6. Notice the headings in the Start menu. You might see Favorites And History, Files, Communications, or other entries, depending on how much data is stored on the computer's hard drive that contains your first name.

Figure 1-3: Type the name of any program, file, folder, favorite, or other item in the Start Search box for instant results.

## SEARCH THE INTERNET

Just as you can search your hard drive from the Start menu, you can search the Internet. Here's how:

1. Click the Start button. It's the round, blue button at the bottom left of the desktop.

2. Type what you're looking for, and click Search The Internet.

From your Web browser, you can immediately scan the results, without having to manually open Windows Internet Explorer 7 in Windows Vista or perform a separate Internet search.

# **Personalization** Features

Oh, what fun it is to browse through backgrounds and screen savers! Knowing that, originally we thought this section should be the first one in this chapter, because it's generally the first task people perform when they get a new computer. In reality, though, getting connected to the Internet and adding a user or two are probably a little more important. That doesn't mean screen savers, backgrounds, display settings, and the like aren't important to you, though! That being said, you'll now learn how to personalize Windows Vista.

## CHANGE THE DESKTOP BACKGROUND

There's no telling what background you have on your desktop right now. That's because someone has to choose it during installation, and there are a lot of options. Therefore, you may want to change what you have displayed right now.

To change your desktop background, follow these steps:

1. Right-click an empty area of the desktop, and select Personalize.

2. In Personalize Appearance And Sounds, click Desktop Background.

3. In the Picture Location drop-down list, select Windows Wallpapers, as shown in Figure 1-4.

4. Use the scroll bar on the right to browse through the pictures.

5. Select a picture.

6. Select how the picture should be positioned. Choices include the following:

   **Fit To Screen**   The picture covers the entire screen.

   **Tile**   The picture is tiled across the screen a number of times.

   **Center**   The picture is centered in the middle of the screen.

7. Click OK.

**TIP** If you have a picture of your own you'd like to use as a desktop background, instead of selecting Windows Wallpapers, click Browse. Locate the picture on your hard drive, and click Open. You can then use that picture as a background.

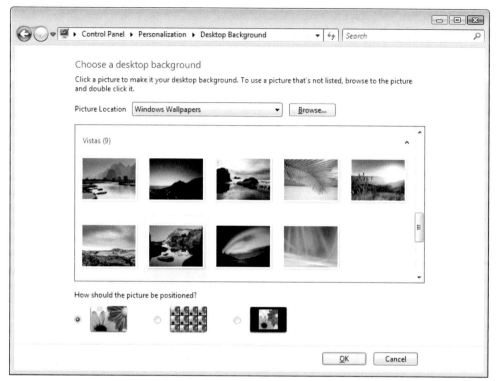

**Figure 1-4:** You have plenty of desktop backgrounds to choose from; select Windows Wallpapers to browse through your options.

## APPLY A SCREEN SAVER

Screen savers used to be an important part of computing. You needed a screen saver to save your screen from image burn-in. In the olden days, if you left your computer on for a long period of time, the image that was showing on the screen would burn into the monitor. This doesn't happen anymore, but that doesn't mean we don't love our screen savers anyway. And now we use screen savers to protect our computers with a password while we're away from it, so screen savers actually do have a valid purpose.

To turn on or change a screen saver, follow these steps:

1. Right-click an empty area of the desktop, and select Properties.

2. In Personalize Appearance And Sounds, click Screen Saver.

③ Click the arrow in the Screen Saver dialog box to view the available screen savers. Select any one of them to view it in the dialog box; click Preview to view it in full-screen mode. (If viewing it in full-screen mode, move the mouse to exit the screen saver.)

④ After selecting a screen saver to apply, type how many minutes the computer should be idle before turning on the screen saver. You can also select On Resume, Display Logon Screen.

⑤ Click Settings, and configure the settings as desired. Not all screen savers have settings.

⑥ Click OK.

## OPTIMIZE THE DISPLAY

Don't go overboard, but do take a look at the Display Settings box. You just may want to change the resolution.

To configure the display properties, follow these steps:

① Right-click an empty area of the desktop, and select Properties.

② In Personalize Appearance And Sounds, click Display Settings.

③ Under Resolution, move the slider to change the resolution of the monitor.

**TIP** Without getting too technical, *resolution* is how many *pixels*, or little squares of color information, appear on your screen. A higher resolution produces a sharper image than a lower one. The higher in resolution you go, the smaller the icons, windows, and other items appearing on your desktop will be. Although it's ultimately a matter of personal preference, try 1024×768 for 15-inch monitors, 1280×1024 for 17- and 19-inch monitors, and 1600×1200 for 20-inch monitors and bigger.

④ Under Colors, click the arrow to configure how many colors to use. The more, the better; choose 32-Bit if it's available.

⑤ Click OK.

# WHAT IS AERO?

You've probably heard the hype about something called Aero. But what is it? In a nutshell, Aero is the ultimate visual experience for Windows Vista. It's a new user interface with a transparent glass design with animations and cool new colors, and it's a feature you can use only if your computer meets some specific requirements.

Aero comes with Windows Vista Business, Windows Vista Enterprise, Windows Vista Home Premium, and Windows Vista Ultimate, but you'll also need to meet some hardware requirements. For starters, this includes a 1-gigahertz (GHz) processor, 1 gigabyte (GB) of random access memory (RAM), and a 128-megabyte (MB) graphics card. Aero also requires a DirectX 9–class graphics processor that supports a Windows Display Driver Model, Pixel Shader 2.0 in hardware, and 32 bits per pixel. You'll need your display settings for color at 32-bit too.

## TURN ON AERO

Come on, you know you want to...turn on Aero, and give it a whirl:

1. Right-click an empty area of the desktop, and click Personalize.

2. Select Windows Color And Appearance.

3. If you see what's shown in the following illustration, you can use the Aero interface. If you see something else, specifically an Appearance Settings dialog box, you don't meet the minimum requirements to run Aero. (This may be because of the edition of Windows Vista you're running or because your computer doesn't meet the minimum requirements.)

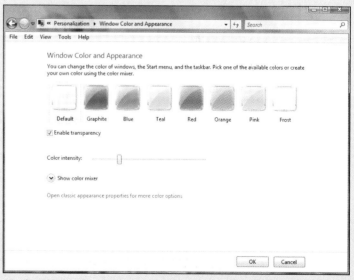

4. Select Enable Transparency.

5. Select a color.

6. Click OK.

You have to be able to access the Windows Color And Appearance screen to turn on Aero. Select Enable Transparency, and select a color to enjoy this awesome new interface enhancement.

# **The** Sidebar **and Gadgets**

The Windows Sidebar offers a place to organize and manage the information you need on a daily basis right from your desktop. We're not talking folders, files, or programs here; we're talking about features such as the current weather, news headlines, up-to-the-minute stock quotes, a calendar, sticky notepads, and the time (down to the second). Windows Vista offers this information in the form of a *gadget*, a mini-program that is continuously updated when you have an always-on Internet connection. Figure 1-5 shows an example of a Sidebar configuration, and Chapter 14 shows you how Sidebar can be a second set of eyes for you.

## TURN ON THE SIDEBAR

To turn on the Sidebar, follow these steps:

1. Click Start, and in the Start Search box type **sidebar**.

2. Under Programs, click Windows Sidebar.

> **TIP** Alternately, to turn on the Windows Sidebar, click Start, All Programs, Accessories, Sidebar.

## CONFIGURE SIDEBAR PROPERTIES

If you like the Sidebar, you need to tell Windows Vista so it can open the Sidebar each time you log on. You also want to state where you want the Sidebar to show on the desktop—the left side or the right and on top of all windows or behind them.

To configure the Sidebar properties, follow these steps:

1. Click Start, and type **sidebar** in the Start Search box.

2. Under Programs, click Windows Sidebar Properties.

3. To have the Sidebar start when Windows starts, select Start Sidebar When Windows Starts.

④ To configure how the Sidebar sits on the desktop, select or clear Sidebar Is Always On Top Of Other Windows.

⑤ To change where the Sidebar appears, select Right or Left. (Right is the default.)

⑥ Click OK.

## ADD, REMOVE, AND CONFIGURE GADGETS

You'll probably want to tell a Sidebar weather gadget what city you live in so you can get weather for your area. The same is true of the time, sports teams you follow, and more. And, you'll find that some gadgets really grab you while others just take up valuable desktop space. With that in mind, you need to know how to add, remove, and configure gadgets.

With the Sidebar on the desktop, follow these steps to remove a gadget:

① To remove a gadget, rest the pointer on the gadget.

② Click the Close button (the X) at the upper right of the gadget.

③ Click Close Gadget.

With the Sidebar on the desktop, follow these steps to add a gadget:

① Move your pointer to the top of the Sidebar, look for Gadgets, and click the plus sign next to it.

② Double-click any gadget to add it; Figure 1-6 shows available gadgets. (You will be able to see only four or five gadgets on the Sidebar at one time because of the limitations of the monitor and screen resolution. If you select more than four or five, you can either drag some of the gadgets off the Sidebar and onto the desktop or delete some gadgets you've previously chosen.)

③ Click the Close button in the upper-right corner of the gadget window to close it.

**Figure 1-5:** The new Sidebar in Windows Vista lets you keep up-to-the-minute news, weather, stock quotes, sports scores, and more, right on your desktop.

**Figure 1-6:**
Windows Vista
comes with several
built-in gadgets
you can add, as
shown here, or
you can go online
to get more from
third parties.

With the Sidebar on the desktop, follow these steps to configure a gadget:

1. Rest the pointer on the gadget to configure.

2. Click the wrench icon on the gadget's right side.

3. Make changes to the gadget by using the gadget's options. (For a weather gadget, type your city name to configure the gadget for your local weather.)

**TROUBLESHOOTING** The only problem you might run across with gadgets is if you choose too many that require online access and you have a slow connection to the Internet. If you have 20 gadgets running and notice that surfing the Internet is a little slower than it used to be, that's why, so you should consider removing some of them.

## EXPLORE FLIP **3D**

With Flip 3D you can quickly preview all your open programs, files, folders, Web sites, photos, and more, by using an awesome new three-dimensional look and feel.

To use Flip 3D, follow these steps:

1. Open several windows. Consider opening the following: a Microsoft Office Word 2007 document, a photo, Internet Explorer 7, and a couple of folders.

2. Hold down the Windows logo key, and press the Tab key once to open Flip 3D.

3. While still holding down the Windows logo key, press the Tab key again to move to the next open window. Repeat this step to see all open windows.

4. To bring any selected window to the forefront, release the Tab key and the Windows logo key. The graphic shows Flip 3D.

Flip 3D offers a visual three-dimensional view of your open applications.

This chapter offered an overview of how to begin using Windows Vista. The first tasks you'll want to do are create additional users, connect to the Internet, and get used to the Start menu, specifically how to access programs and files. You'll also want to personalize Windows Vista and learn about the new features available in the interface. Having mastered all that, you can now move on to Chapter 2!

- "Clean house" first, and transfer only the data you need from your old PC

- Adhere to the built-in system for saving files

- Create a system that allows for easy and daily backups

- Create and use a search folder to keep data easy to find

# **Set Up** Windows Vista, and Create an Organizational System

# CHAPTER 2

Think about what it's like to move into a new home or apartment. (Caution: analogy coming!) Your new space has so much potential, and you have so many ideas to make the place comfortable, organized, uncluttered, and user-friendly. The layout of the place helps you get started too; for instance, you know you should put beds in the bedrooms; sofas and recliners in the living areas; and stereos, game stations, and TVs in the media room.

You need to look at your new Windows Vista operating system–based PC the same way. Before moving anything in, get rid of stuff you don't want or need, look at the layout of the hard drive and

*Take a little extra time at first, and you can create a livable, breathable, adaptable, and expandable computer experience.*

decide what you want to (and really should) put where, and make sure you can expand your organizational structure with your needs in the future (in a home, perhaps by adding bookshelves; in Windows Vista, perhaps by creating subfolders). Take a little extra time at first, and you can create a livable, breathable, adaptable, and expandable computer experience (just like a home).

# Transfer Data with Windows Easy Transfer

In the olden days, we actually rather dreaded buying a new computer. It was a hassle to set it up and get it just right. It took days, if not weeks. You had to call your Internet service provider (ISP) and ask for the settings to connect to the Internet. And then you had to call them back when you couldn't figure out how to do it yourself. You had to call them again because you could send an e-mail but not receive one. You had to export and then import Microsoft Internet Explorer Favorites, create new user accounts, somehow bring over the address book and e-mail messages, and one way or another copy all your personal data. No more. Windows Easy Transfer, which comes with Windows Vista, lets you to transfer all of this and more with no problem at all (and no calling your ISP).

**NOTE** The old computer must be running Windows XP or Windows Vista to use Windows Easy Transfer.

### CLEAN UP THE OLD COMPUTER

 **1 to 3 hours**

Before you move to a new home, you put the trash out on the curb. You don't carry it with you and find a place for it in your new home. You do the same with furniture you don't want as well as items that are damaged. You should do the same with the data you transfer. Just as with moving houses, you should first clean up and get rid of everything you no longer need or want so you don't clutter up your new PC with it.

To get rid of the junk on your old PC, do all of the following:

- Delete pictures, videos, music, data, and other media you no longer want.

- Delete (or back up to CD or DVD) old work documents, spreadsheets, grocery lists, to-do lists, and other unnecessary personal files.

- Clean up Microsoft Outlook Express (or Microsoft Office Outlook) by deleting unwanted saved e-mail and e-mail folders you created but no longer need, the items in Sent Items, and the items in Deleted Items. Be extremely vigilant about e-mails that contain attachments.

- Clean up Internet Explorer. Delete Favorites you no longer access, and orga- nize what's left. Click File, Export to export and save cookies (Windows Easy Transfer doesn't get those). Delete temporary files.

- Use Disk Cleanup to get rid of other unwanted files.

- Restart the computer, and then empty the Recycle Bin.

> **TIP** Make sure you have the product activation codes for any software you own, as well as the CDs. If you downloaded software and don't have a CD, burn the program files to a CD before wiping the hard drive clean.

## START WINDOWS EASY TRANSFER ON THE NEW COMPUTER

 **30 minutes**

You could be in one of two situations. Either you have two computers, an old PC and a new one (yay!), or you have one older PC you want to upgrade to Windows Vista with a clean installation. (If you upgrade a computer to Windows Vista without performing a clean installation, you won't have to do any of this, because all your files and settings will remain intact.) Here, we're assuming you have two computers—an old one and a new one.

> **TIP** If you have only one computer, read the instructions here, and then read the "What If the Old Computer and New Computer Are the Same Computer?" sidebar. You can still use Windows Easy Transfer; the process is just a bit different.

To start the process of transferring files and settings from your old PC your new PC, follow these steps:

1. On the new PC, click Start, and in the Start Search box type **Windows Easy Transfer**.

2. Click Windows Easy Transfer, listed under Programs, to open it, as shown in Figure 2-1.

**Figure 2-1:** Windows Easy Transfer can help you transfer just about everything.

3. Click Next to start Windows Easy Transfer.

4. Select Start A New Transfer.

5. Click My New Computer.

6. If you have an Easy Transfer cable, select Yes, I Have An Easy Transfer Cable, and follow the directions on the following screen to connect it. If you do not have an Easy Transfer cable, select No, Show Me More Options. An Easy Transfer cable connects two computers by using their universal serial bus (USB) ports.

7. Windows Easy Transfer needs to be installed on the old computer. When prompted, select from the following:

   • Yes, I Installed It

- Yes, My Old Computer Is Running Windows Vista

- No, I Need To Install It Now

**8** If you chose one of the first two options in the previous step, skip to step 9. If you chose the third option, select one of the following to install Windows Easy Transfer on your old computer (you'll see instructions for how to do this after you make your choice):

- CD

- USB Flash Drive

- External Hard Disk Or Shared Network Folder

- Windows Installation Disk Or Windows Easy Transfer CD

**9** Select Yes or No when asked whether your computer is connected to a network. If you select Yes, you can save the transfer information to a network drive. If you select No, you'll next need to select from CD, DVD, or Removable Media.

**10** When asked whether you have a Windows Easy Transfer key, select No, I Need A Key. Write down the key.

## CONTINUE WINDOWS EASY TRANSFER ON THE OLD COMPUTER

**25 minutes**

Make your way to the old computer, key in hand. Start Windows Easy Transfer on the old computer, and then follow these steps:

**1** Click Start, and in the Start Search box type **Windows Easy Transfer**. (Alternately, you can insert the Windows Vista CD or start Windows Easy Transfer in any alternate way you chose earlier, including from a network drive.)

**2** Click Next to start Windows Easy Transfer.

**3** Select Start A New Transfer.

④ Click My Old Computer.

⑤ If you have an Easy Transfer cable, select Yes, I Have An Easy Transfer Cable, and follow the directions on the following screen to connect it. If you do not have an Easy Transfer cable, select No, Show Me More Options.

What happens next includes too many scenarios to detail. It's not hard, though; you have to merely choose where you're going to save the data to transfer. It may be that you select a network drive, burn a CD or DVD, or use an external drive. Whichever you choose, you'll have to browse to a location to save the information. Remember, it has to be a location both computers can connect to and access. We prefer a network drive or external drive, a place that both computers have access to already.

Once you're prompted to save your data, you're almost done. You need to select only what you want to transfer. Select from the following:

- All User Accounts, Files, And Settings

- My User Account, Files, And Settings

- Advanced Options

If you select either of the first two, you're just about set. Select the first if you have multiple users and accounts or the second if it's all about you. However, we suggest selecting Advanced Options. With this option, you get to pick what you want to transfer and what you don't.

To complete the process, follow these steps:

① In the Advanced Options dialog box, select the files, folders, and settings to transfer. Remember to get all your personal data; you may have to browse to find it all. Click Next.

② Type a user name for the new computer. Click Next.

③ Wait, and do not use either computer until the transfer is complete.

④ Click Close on both computers.

# WHAT IF THE OLD COMPUTER AND NEW COMPUTER ARE THE SAME COMPUTER?

If you did not purchase a new computer but instead want to do a clean installation of an older Windows XP computer by using a Windows Vista CD, you can still use Windows Easy Transfer. You'll work through the process as detailed in the previous section, with a few minor changes.

You'll still start Windows Easy Transfer on your single computer (by using the Windows Vista CD), select a new transfer as detailed, and then, instead of selecting My New Computer as shown in step 5, select My Old Computer.

Work through the process. Once you've chosen which files and settings to transfer and you've saved the data to an external drive, you'll then install Windows Vista on the PC and run Windows Easy Transfer again. After installing Windows Vista, you'll select Continue A Transfer In Progress and, when prompted, browse to the location of the saved file.

## LOCATE TRANSFERRED DATA

You'll find the transferred data where you expect to find it. You'll find your documents in the Documents folder, your pictures in the Pictures folder, and your music in the Music folder. Just as you would not expect the moving helpers to put the bedroom suite in the kitchen or the washer and dryer in the foyer, you would not expect Windows Easy Transfer to put your data in the wrong area!

# Use the Windows Vista Folder and File System

Okay, we're sure we've made our point. Put stuff where it belongs, and you'll not only have a sense of normalcy but you'll also always know where to find the stuff you want. With that in mind, you should always adhere to the built-in system for saving data already created in Windows Vista. We'll give you the leeway to create subfolders, but come on, you wouldn't store your blender and food processor in the bathroom, so don't save your pictures to the C: drive or your music to the desktop!

## GET THE MOST FROM THE BUILT-IN SYSTEM FOR SAVING DATA

**20 minutes**

The built-in Windows Vista file system includes folders such as Documents, Pictures, Videos, and Music. It also has Public Documents, Public Pictures, Public Downloads, Public Music, Recorded TV, Public Video, and similar folders. The first list includes private folders, and the second one includes public ones. These folders are where you want to save your files.

> **TIP** Save your personal data to your personal folders; save data to share in the public folders. Saving data that everyone accesses in the public folders reduces duplicate data on the hard drive.

To make sure you always have access to these folders, consider putting them on the desktop:

1. Right-click an empty area of the desktop, and click Personalize.

2. Under Tasks on the left side in the Personalization window, select Change Desktop Icons.

3. As shown in Figure 2-2, select the User's Files check box.

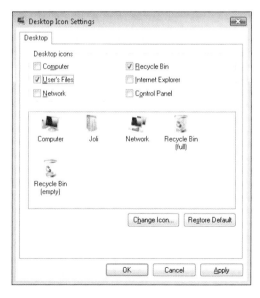

Figure 2-2: Adding your personal folder to the desktop makes it easier to access (and back up).

④ Click OK, and close the Desktop Icons Settings dialog box.

⑤ Open your personal folder. It will be the folder with your name on it. Notice the subfolders inside your personal folder, as shown in Figure 2-3.

⑥ Right-click the Start menu, and click Explore All Users.

⑦ Resize the window so you can access the desktop behind it. (If the window is maximized, click Restore Down in the top-right corner. Resize the window by dragging from any corner or side.)

⑧ Locate the Public folder.

⑨ Right-click that folder, drag it to the desktop, release the mouse, and then click Create Shortcut Here. Conversely, you can simply drag the item to the desktop, and the shortcut will be created automatically.

You can now access the folders you need right from the desktop. And, when clicking File, Save As, you need to select only the desktop, which is near the top of the list, as shown in Figure 2-4, and select the folder and subfolder you need.

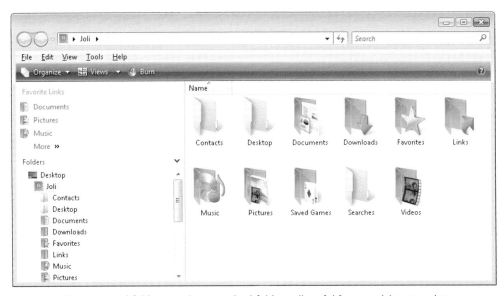

Figure 2-3: Your personal folder contains several subfolders, all useful for organizing your data.

**Figure 2-4:** The next time you save anything, click Save As, Desktop, and then select the folder or subfolder you need.

## CREATE YOUR OWN FOLDERS AND SUBFOLDERS

You can create your own folders and subfolders quite easily. You don't have to settle for what's in Windows Vista. First, think of a folder or subfolder you currently need, and decide where it should ultimately be placed. If you have a lot of pictures, for instance, you may want to create subfolders in the Pictures folder for each month of each year or to separate images by category (vacations, kids, pets, and so on). For the Video folder, you may want to do the same.

You may ultimately decide to create entirely new folders. Here are some ideas for new folders and ideas for organizing subfolders:

**Scans**   Create subfolders for the year the image was originally taken, what side of the family the picture belongs with, or images you want to use in a virtual scrapbook or photo story.

**Podcasts**   Create subfolders by category of podcast, genre, or content.

**My Movies**   Create subfolders for project files and completed files, photo stories, and files saved for specific types of media (such as files you've burned to DVDs).

**Projects**   Create subfolders for ongoing projects that aren't finished and aren't ready for any other folder such as digitizing your picture library, transferring video from old VHS tapes, creating movies from videos, and so on.

**Artwork**   Create subfolders for digital artwork, scrapbook ideas, and scanned images from your children's art class.

**Work Projects**   Create subfolders for project names, months of the year, client, or due date.

**Clients**   Create subfolders for each client, and include each client's personal files and folders.

**5 minutes**

To create a folder and a subfolder, follow these steps:

1. From the desktop or from the Start menu, open your personal user folder. It's the folder with your name on it.

2. Right-click an empty area of the right pane, and click New, Folder.

3. Type a name for the folder, and press Enter.

4. Open the folder, and repeat steps 1, 2, and 3 to create a subfolder inside the new one.

## MOVE DATA TO SUBFOLDERS

Now it's time to get down and dirty with it. No matter what mess you had on your old computer and no matter whether you had put pictures in your Documents folder, had kept videos on the C: drive, or had downloaded files to the desktop, we're going to straighten it out here. And, if you have a new pristine PC, you'll learn how to keep it that way.

**10 minutes to no telling how long**

Here's how to get started moving data to the proper place on your hard drive (and saving new data there):

① Open your personal folder. Look inside the first subfolder, and verify that what's inside is what's supposed to be there.

② If you see anything in the folder you no longer want, right-click the item, and click Delete. You'll have to verify you want to do this by clicking Yes.

③ If you see anything out of place, right-click the item, and click Cut.

④ Click Back, and select the folder in which the item belongs. If you don't have a folder for it, create one.

⑤ Once inside the proper folder, right-click, and click Paste.

⑥ Continue doing this until the files and folders are in their proper places.

> **TIP** To select contiguous files, hold down the Shift key, and select the first and last in the list. To select noncontiguous files, hold down the Ctrl key while selecting.

You can also right-click while dragging files and folders, and when you release the mouse, you can click Move to move the selected files. (If you mess up, click Organize, Undo.)

## New Search Features

The search folder feature is a powerful new tool that makes it easy to locate and organize your files. Although we've stressed the importance of keeping your data organized the old-fashioned way, in the default folders and personal subfolders, even if you can't or don't want to do that, you'll still be okay. With the new search features in Windows Vista and by employing a search folder, you really don't need to have a clue about where something is, as long as you know a bit about what you want to find.

## LOCATE A FILE WITH SEARCH

For instance, say you copied some pictures from your digital camera last June when your nephew graduated from high school but you don't see those pictures in the Pictures folder or any subfolders. Now you need to find them, for whatever reason— maybe to prove to someone you really did go to the event.

**5 minutes**

Here's what you can do:

1. Click Start, and click Search.

2. In the Search Results window, select Picture, as shown in Figure 2-5.

3. Type **Graduation** to see whether the desired results are shown. If not, search for June, the month the pictures were taken, or your nephew's name.

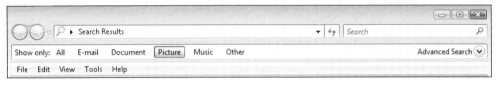

Figure 2-5:
To search for a specific type of data, select it from the Show Only choices.

Chances are, you'll find what you want. However, you can always use advanced searching, which we'll cover next.

## PERFORM AN ADVANCED SEARCH

Advanced searches let you further define what you need to find. To view advanced options, click Start, click Search, and then expand Advanced Search, as shown in Figure 2-6.

Figure 2-6:
View Advanced Search options in the Search Results window.

Options for advanced searching include the following:

**Location**   Choose from Everywhere, Indexed Locations, Computer, Local Hard Drives, My Sharing Folders, Local Disk, and additional options. If you can remember where you may have saved the file, this is a good place to start.

**Date**   Choose from Date, Date Modified, Date Created, and Date Accessed. Once you select criteria here, you can then choose to search for any dates or dates on, prior to, or after a specific date. If you can remember when you created the file or last modified it, this is a good place to start.

**Size (KB)**   Choose Any, Equals, Is Less Than, or Is Greater Than, and type a specific size. If the file is extremely large, such as a video, this is a good place to start.

**Name**   Search for a specific file name (or part of one). If you know the file name contains the word *widget*, this is a good place to start.

**Tags**   Search by using a tag. If you've added tags manually and you remember what those tags are, this is a good place to start.

**Authors**   Search by using a specific author name. If you remember who wrote or created the file, this is a good place to start.

> **TIP** Don't forget to click Search when you're finished setting criteria.

## SAVE A SEARCH FOLDER

Once you've found the results you want, you can save the folder for future reference. For instance, let's say you finally came across those graduation pictures and you found them by searching through the month of June 2006. You couldn't find them earlier because when you uploaded them from your camera, you named the folder Camera Pictures III, or something equally nondescript. To save the results so you can access them next time (and so any other pictures that have to do with any other graduations may eventually end up there), follow the steps on the next page.

**5 minutes**

① Click Save Search.

② In the Save As dialog box, click Browse Folders if it's available so that what you see is what's shown in Figure 2-7.

③ Type a memorable file name, such as **John's Graduation** or **Graduation**.

④ Verify Save As Type is Search Folder.

⑤ Select a folder under Favorite Links to save the search folder. You may want to save a search folder full of pictures to the Pictures folder. Whatever you choose, may sure it's something that makes sense and is one of the default folders.

⑥ Click Save.

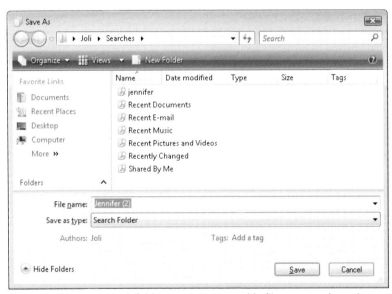

Figure 2-7: To save a search folder, create a memorable file name, and save it to a folder that represents the data in it.

# USE SMART SEARCHES FOR EVERYTHING

Okay, okay. Maybe you're one of *those* people. You don't know where your blender is, and to be honest, you don't care. You're just tickled pink that it's not in your way while you're making a sandwich. If someone wants margaritas while at your house, they're going to have to find the blender themselves (it may be in the garage) or bring their own. You just can't stay organized. Your mind doesn't work that way.

We'll assume you hardly ever remember to browse to the correct folder to save music, pictures, videos, and data. We'll also assume you are fully aware you have stuff scattered across your entire hard drive and you're sick of being harassed about it. You usually use a program's Recently Opened list or the Start menu's Recent Items list to find what you want, and that generally works well. Okay, okay.

Here's what you do: Name data appropriately. Give videos names that describe them. Give pictures names that detail the subject or date. Name Microsoft Office Word documents with a word or two that describes them. Assign tags and keywords if you can. Then, anytime you want to find something, create a search from the Start menu, and if you find what you want, save the results as a search folder. Name the folder appropriately, and save that folder to your desktop. Now, all you have to do is open the folder to find all the files, even new ones, that match the search criteria for it.

This chapter gave you an overview of how to get organized and stay organized with Windows Vista. You learned how to transfer data from an old PC, without wrecking your new one; how to use and adhere to the built-in file and folder structure in Windows Vista; how to create a file system that is backup-friendly; and how to use Search and search folders to find data that has gone missing.

# PART II Pictures

- **Scan old photos**
- **Create a working system for uploading and managing digital pictures**
- **Create picture metadata for ultimate sorting and organization**
- **Group images in search folders for better management**
- **Use your favorite images as screen savers and desktop backgrounds**

# **Construct** an Amazing
Photo Library

# CHAPTER 3

It's time to get organized, get creative, and construct a photo library you can be proud of! C'mon, the dark ages of shoeboxes and sticky-paged photo albums are over, and, we hope, so is showing your latest pictures to others from the preview screen of your digital camera (or worse, your cell phone).

You owe it to yourself to create a digital library you will actually use and enjoy. You deserve a library that makes showing slide shows on your PC (with music to boot) as easy as turning on the television; that includes picture folders named Graduation, Trip to Italy, Kids, The Band, Beer Parties, and Bucky the Kat so you can easily access what you want; and that includes folders and subfolders just the right size to create an awesome DVD or CD of pictures when you want to share them with family far away.

*It's time to get organized, get creative, and construct a photo library you can be proud of!*

You also owe it to yourself to use the new search folders in the Windows Vista operating system. Search folders offer a new twist to organizing data. Although you can stick with the old folder/subfolder routine, you can opt to switch to a search folder strategy for even easier organization. Search folders are "live" and change as the data on your PC changes. Just create a search for specific pictures based on their metadata, such as the month the picture was taken, and then save the search as a search folder, and you're off and running with an awesome new organizational structure. Every time you open that particular folder, from now until your computer poops out, Windows Vista automatically updates the folder with the latest images that match the criteria you set for the folder when you created it.

# Scan Old Photos (or Pay to Have Them Scanned)

We all have boxes of photos we cherish. Unfortunately, we generally have too many to even know what to do with (and that even includes putting them into albums), and we have way too many to consider scanning. However, scanning is really the only way to preserve your memories safely. As you know, physical pictures deteriorate over time, just like AHS and reel-to-reel tapes. It's just no good to keep your prized possessions boxed up in an attic or basement. Not only will they go south sooner, but you can't even enjoy them while they last.

### DECIDE WHAT PICTURES TO SCAN

 **The time it takes to drink a large coffee**

You most likely can't commit to scanning all the old photos you have. The task seems too overwhelming. That's okay. However, you can commit to spending one Saturday setting up your scanner and converting 10 or so of your favorites. And if you can commit to that, we know that you'll be more likely to scan a few more photos next weekend and the weekend after that, and perhaps after a while, you'll actually have all your photos safely scanned (and backed up to DVDs). With that as a positive result in your mind, grab a couple of boxes from the basement or attic, and start going through them. Pick your favorites and the ones in the most need of attention. Here's what to look for when going through your old photos:

- Photos you haven't seen in years, those you miss seeing, and those that mean a lot to you or members of your family.

- Photos of deceased relatives or pets.

- "Generational" photos; those photos taken of multiple generations in a single shot.

- Photos on the verge of deterioration. You can edit and digitally remaster them to bring them back to life.

## CHOOSE THE RIGHT SCANNER

Once you know what pictures you want to preserve, you'll need the right scanner for the job. Not all scanners are up to the task. Here's what to look for in a scanner:

- Make sure the scanner you are planning to use can scan 4-by-6-inch, 5-by-7-inch, and 8-by-10-inch prints.

- Understand that a scanner that connects to a FireWire port will operate much faster than one using a USB port. Look at your computer to see what ports are available, and purchase and connect a scanner accordingly.

- If you want to scan negatives and other types of media, verify the scanner you're planning to use has the appropriate adapters available. Better yet, purchase a specialty printer that can handle the job more easily.

- Install the scanner's software, and learn how to use it.

> **NOTE** If you have negatives or slides you'd like to preserve, you'll need a scanner capable of scanning them. If that's the case, look for a film scanner. Film scanners let you feed your film and negatives in directly, making the job much easier while at the same time producing better results than you'd get from a flatbed scanner.

## SCAN YOUR PICTURES

 **It depends on how many images you want to scan, but plan for about 20 minutes for the first one and less for the rest.**

When you're ready to scan, place your first photo in the scanner. Press whatever button is required on the scanner to start it. When prompted, select your scanner software from the list of choices to launch the scanner. Work through the software to set up and create the scan. You can directly import scanned photos by using Windows Photo Gallery, too. Once finished, save the scan to a subfolder in Pictures named Scans. You'll need to create the Scans folder, and we'll talk about that shortly.

Here are a few tips for getting the best scans possible:

* Always use the Preview button before scanning to see whether the image is aligned properly.

* Choose the correct color mode for the image. If it's a black-and-white image, choose the black-and-white setting, for instance.

* Make sure the scanner glass is clean.

* Always scan at least at 300 dots per inch (dpi). If you want to scan an image and then create a print of it that's larger than the original, scan at a higher setting, at least 600 dpi. You'll have to experiment with your scanner to find the perfect settings.

* Explore scanner settings that automatically remove scratches and blotches in the scan.

**TIP** No matter how many pictures you scan, whether it's five or five hundred, back them up to an external hard drive, a CD, or a DVD as soon as possible.

# PAY SOMEONE ELSE TO SCAN YOUR PICTURES

Several online companies are in the business of scanning old photos, transferring old videos, and so on, to CDs and DVDs. They'll even do a bit of image editing for you. One of these companies is DigMyPics at *www.digmypics.com*, which can do as few as 1 photo or as many as 2,000. If you have fewer than 500 photos to scan, each scan is about $.50 US. DigMyPics also does 35-millimeter film scanning. If you have a lot of photos to scan and a little extra cash, this may be a better option.

## SAVE THE SCANS IN AN ORGANIZATIONAL WONDERLAND

 **10 minutes for the first save, less for future saves**

Once you've created a scan with your scanner and its software, you'll need to create a working folder for saving and organizing your scans. Here's how:

1. Click the File (or related) menu, and then click Save As in the program in which you're working. Generally, the File menu is the first menu available at the top of the menu bar on the left side. If the program you're working in doesn't have such a menu, look for a Save As option.

2. In the Save As dialog box, browse to the Pictures folder.

3. Right-click in the Pictures folder, and click New, Folder. You may also see a command called Create New Folder or something similar.

4. Type **Scans** to name the new folder, and click to open it.

5. Inside the Scans folder, right-click again, and then click New, Folder. Then name that folder appropriately; in other words, type a subfolder name that represents what's inside the folder.

6. Save the first scan there.

As you progress through the pictures to scan, save the scanned images to sub-folders in the Scans folder. Create as many subfolders as needed to organize the folder's contents.

# Create a Good System for Transferring Pictures from Your Digital Camera

 30 minutes

The next step in creating a working and expandable digital picture library is to create a system for transferring pictures from your digital camera. Windows Vista makes it pretty easy by prompting you with options each time you connect your camera, but you still need to create a system that works for you.

> **NOTE** Before you start, make sure your camera is installed properly.

The best way to create and maintain an effective digital library is to transfer your pictures from your camera to the PC the same day you take them and then delete them from the camera. The reason you should adopt this strategy is threefold:

- Your camera's memory will never get full, and you'll never miss that perfect shot because you don't have any room left on your camera's memory card.

- Every time you upload pictures to your PC, they will be (almost always) of one subject, such as a graduation, a camping trip, a new home, or a concert and resulting party. When uploading, you can thus name the folder you create for the pictures appropriately, and all the pictures in the folder will be of the same event or topic.

- Deleting the images from your camera after uploading them leaves you prepared for the next event and solves the problem of uploading duplicate images onto your PC (which is disorganized and a waste of hard drive space). You will have duplicate images if you do not delete the images from your camera.

If you follow our advice here, you'll see quite quickly how this plan works. The pictures you put on your PC will be organized the moment you upload them. They'll be in suitable folders. There will be no duplicates and no long wait while, say, 300 pictures upload when instead you wanted only the three new ones on the camera.

## USE WINDOWS PHOTO GALLERY TO INITIATE THE FIRST TRANSFER

**10 minutes**

Windows Vista has everything you need to upload pictures from your digital camera. You will no longer have to fumble around with clumsy third-party software just to do basic tasks with your images. Windows Photo Gallery, which comes with Windows Vista, offers all you need.

To initiate a transfer with Windows Photo Gallery, follow these steps:

1. Connect your digital camera to the appropriate port on your PC. Generally, this is a USB port. If nothing happens, turn the camera on, and make sure it's on the playback setting or set up as directed by the camera's documentation.

2. When prompted, click Import Pictures, as shown in Figure 3-1.

3. When the Importing Pictures And Videos window opens, you'll be prompted to tag these pictures. Type a name that represents the group of pictures you're importing. Then, click Options.

4. The Import Settings dialog box appears, as shown in Figure 3-2. Configure the options as desired. In Folder Name, we prefer Tag + Date Imported. In this case, the folder name will be the tag you typed in step 3, followed by today's date.

**Figure 3-1:** Windows Vista comes with all you need to start and complete the import process.

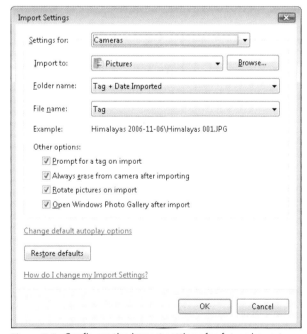

**Figure 3-2:** Configure the import settings for future import processes.

⑤ For File Name, we prefer Tag. In this case, each picture is given a name (its tag name) followed by a number. You'll see an example of how your choice will look in the Example line.

⑥ Select Always Erase From Camera After Importing if you desire. It is not selected by default. If you don't select it, you can erase the images during the import process. Deleting from the camera occurs after the import process.

⑦ Click OK and OK again. (If you've made changes to the import options, Windows Photo Gallery will restart, and you'll need to type the tag again.) Click Import.

⑧ Windows Photo Gallery opens, and the imported pictures appear at the top of Windows Photo Gallery in the Recently Imported folder.

However, you'll also notice in the list of folders in the left pane that Windows Vista has created a new folder in the Tags section of Windows Photo Gallery. You'll learn more about that later.

# RETRIEVE YOUR ONLINE PICTURES

Lots of folks put pictures on various Web sites, such as their own personal site or a third-party site such as MySpace or Facebook. The pictures you've posted online should also reside somewhere on your own computer for backup. If they don't, you'll need to get those back so you can have them in your own personal digital library.

To do that, you'll need to first find where the data is stored online. Check out your personal Web pages as well as online photo stores where you may have posted prints. If you have pictures on a Web site, access the site, right-click the image, choose Save Picture As, and make a copy of it on your own PC. It won't be a great photo, because most photos used online are quite small, but at least you'll have a copy.

# Organize with **Windows Photo Gallery**

You can view your pictures by using Windows Photo Gallery. Of course, you can view them in lots of other ways too, but Windows Photo Gallery comes with Windows Vista and is a great application to use. With Windows Photo Gallery you can view all your pictures and videos (or only one or the other); view large thumbnails of pictures without having to open them in a separate window; find pictures by their tag; search by file extension, date, or rating; and more.

To get the most out of Windows Photo Gallery, though, you have to know how to navigate the interface as well as how to create metatags and sort and group the data you have into working folders.

## GROUP AND VIEW IMAGES

**30 minutes**

Start by navigating to the Windows Photo Gallery interface. In this example, you'll learn how to set up the gallery, and armed with that knowledge, you'll then be able to make better decisions regarding how to name future picture folders, how to group images, and how to sort through them to find what you want.

As you might guess, you can find a specific image in Windows Photo Gallery in multiple ways. You can look under All Pictures, under Recently Imported, under Tags, under Date Taken, under Ratings, and under Folders. To learn more, follow these steps:

1. Open Windows Photo Gallery. One way to do this is to click Start, type **Windows Photo Gallery** in the Start Search box, and then click its name when it appears in the Programs list.

2. Click All Pictures And Videos. Windows Photo Gallery lists all the pictures and videos from latest to earliest by year.

3. Under All Pictures And Videos, click Pictures. Only the pictures will appear.

4. Click Recently Imported. Only the pictures recently imported will appear. Figure 3-3 shows an example.

5. Click Tags. All pictures will appear, grouped by their tags. If you've imported pictures and created a tag name, you'll see them here, grouped by that name. You'll also see a lot of images that come with Windows Vista.

Continue in this manner to view what's grouped by Date Taken, Ratings, and Folders. Under Folders, you'll see any folders you've created in the Pictures folder, as well as the Public Pictures, Public Videos, Sample Pictures, and Sample Videos categories. You'll find that Tags and Folders are the best place to locate a picture or a group of pictures.

**NOTE** When you see a picture in multiple folders, such as Recently Imported, Tags, and All Pictures And Videos, note that there are not duplicates of the images in each of these folders. Rather, they're virtual. Windows Photo Gallery does not create duplicates or triplicates; instead, it creates multiple links to the same image so you can access it from within the folder that matches the criteria for it.

**Figure 3-3:** Windows Photo Gallery offers lots of default folders with images already in them, such as this folder, Recently Imported.

## INCORPORATE METADATA

30 minutes

For the pictures you scan and upload to appear in the appropriate folders, you have to create metadata for them. *Metadata* includes the tag name you created when uploading, but it can be so much more. For instance, you can add metadata that includes ratings, months and years, comments, events, people, and even titles and subject names. Once you add the metadata, you can then create and save search folders by using that criteria for even easier access.

For example, if you have a group of pictures tagged New York but some of the pictures are from a class reunion, some are from a wedding, and some are of your relatives, you can add tags or metadata to separate them from the rest of the items in the folder. You can then narrow down a search for a specific image by searching for pictures not just of your trip to New York but those specifically related to the class reunion you attended while you were there.

Here's how to create metadata:

1.  Open Windows Photo Gallery.

2.  Open a folder that contains pictures to which you want to add metadata.

3.  Select a single picture, or select multiple pictures by holding down the Shift key to select contiguous pictures or by holding down the Ctrl key to select noncontiguous ones.

4.  With the pictures selected, right-click, and click Properties.

5.  Do some or all of the following:

    *   Click Title in the picture's Properties dialog box, and type a title.

    *   Click Subject, and type a subject.

    *   Click Rating, and select a rating from one to five stars.

    *   Click Tags to add tags to identify the image. You can add multiple tags if separated by semicolons.

6.  Continue to add information as warranted including date acquired, authors, and so on. Scroll through the list to see the additional properties. You'll see information regarding what camera you used to take the picture, the image size, the file type, the owner, and more. Click OK when finished.

As noted earlier, you can now perform a search for the proper metadata and save the results in a search folder; the next time you want access to that data, it'll be right at your fingertips.

# Create and Save Search Folders

A *search folder* is a folder you create with criteria you select. For instance, you can use the Search feature in Windows Vista to search for only those pictures that have specific metadata, such as a child's name or a date.

To create a basic search for pictures and to see how search folders work, follow these steps:

1. Click Start, Search.

2. In Show Only, click Picture.

3. In the Start Search box, type anything that relates to the pictures you'd like to see, such as **Vacation**, **Pets**, **Kids**, or something similar. Press Enter.

   Figure 3-4 shows the results of us searching for *Jennifer*. Our results offer four pictures. The search does not offer documents with the word *Jennifer* in them, and it doesn't offer music with the word *Jennifer* in the title. It does not display e-mail either. Creating a search just for photos offers results only for photos.

**Figure 3-4:** The Windows Vista new Search feature lets you search for and then save the results to a search folder.

④ You can now save the search into a search folder. The search folder will be a living, breathing (so to speak) being. If, for instance, you take some more pictures of Jennifer, add them to the library, and tag them with the word *Jennifer*, the next time you open this saved folder, you'll see those photos as well as the others already saved. That's because each time you open a saved search folder, Windows Vista updates it!

To save a search, follow these steps:

① Click Save Search in the Search window.

② Name the folder appropriately.

③ Make sure Save As is set to Search Folder.

④ Under Favorite Links, browse to Pictures.

⑤ Click Save.

From now on, each time you want to view pictures matching that particular criteria, you can, just by accessing that search folder.

# PEEK AT WHAT'S TO COME

You'll learn lots more about pictures in the next couple of chapters, but for now, how about taking a peek at what's to come? Think about your favorite picture, and then set it as your desktop background:

① Locate the picture to use as your desktop background from the Pictures folder or wherever it is stored on your hard drive.

② Right-click the image, and click Set As Desktop Background.

- E-mail single and multiple pictures

- Burn pictures to CDs and DVDs

- Create a slide show on a DVD you can play on your TV

- Get photos printed at an online store

# **Share** Your Photos

# CHAPTER 4

Admit it—you've shown pictures and videos to people directly from your digital camera. "Look, there's Junior kicking the winning goal at the soccer match! See?" Well, actually, no, because the viewing screen on your digital camera is 2 inches by 3 inches. Stop the madness! It's time to learn how to share your images with others without making them peer at the tiny screen on your digital camera or phone. In this chapter, you'll learn lots of ways to share your digital photos and videos.

# E-Mail Your Pictures

5 minutes

One of the most common ways to share pictures is to e-mail them. E-mail is fast and easy, and you can share your pictures with a lot of people at once. Although you can send pictures via e-mail in many ways, here you'll learn how to incorporate the e-mailing features of the Windows Vista operating system, namely, Windows Mail.

*It's time to learn how to share your images with others without making them peer at the tiny screen on your digital camera or phone.*

To send a single picture or multiple pictures by using Windows Vista and Windows Mail, follow these steps:

1. Open the Pictures folder and then the subfolder that contains the pictures you want to e-mail.

2. Select each picture you want to send by clicking it once.

3. Right-click one of the selected pictures, click Send To, and then click Mail Recipient.

4. You'll see five options in the Attach Files dialog box that appears, listed here:

   - Smaller: 640×480

   - Small: 800×600

   - Medium: 1024×768

   - Large: 1280×1024

   - Original Size

   Note that selecting any of these options also details the size of the attachment. Many ISPs limit the size of an e-mail to less than 2MB, so a good rule of thumb is for the attachment not to exceed 1.75MB. (Anything in the kilobyte range is okay.) Figure 4-1 shows an example; for more information about selecting the correct option, refer to Table 4-1.

5. Type the recipient's e-mail address, a subject, and a message, and then click Send.

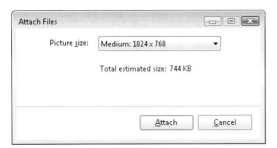

**Figure 4-1:** Use the Attach Files dialog box to help you choose the right size of attachment. Click Attach to attach the file to the email.

| ATTACHMENT OPTION | WHEN TO SELECT |
|---|---|
| Smaller: 640×480 | Select this option when sending a large group of pictures and also when you want to keep the size of one attachment manageable and less than 2MB. Also select this option if the recipient is using a dial-up connection. |
| Small: 800×600 | Select this option when sending a large group of pictures, when you want to keep the size of the attachment manageable and less than 2MB, and when you know the recipient has an older computer and probably has the screen resolution on the computer set to 800×600. Also select this option if the recipient is using a dial-up connection. |
| Medium: 1024×768 | Try this option first, because it is the default, and verify the size of the attachment. If the attachment is less than 1.5MB and you know your recipient does not use a dial-up connection, select it. If the recipient is using dial-up, select Small: 800×600 or Smaller: 640×480. |
| Large: 1280×1024 | Select this option if you have taken and must send a high-quality photo and you know the recipient has a broadband connection to the Internet. If sending multiple pictures produces an attachment that's more than 2MB, consider sending the images separately or compressing them before sending. |
| Original Size | Select this option if the size of the attachment is manageable and you want to send the original picture without changing its size. |

**Table 4-1:** Selecting the correct attachment option

## COMPRESS A GROUP OF IMAGES BEFORE E-MAILING

If you try to send a group of pictures via e-mail but find the size of the attachment to be too large to send in the quality and format you want, you can compress the pictures prior to e-mailing them. Compressing a folder of images can reduce its size. We're not promising miracles here, and some types of data compress better than others, but compressing does reduce file size, even if it's only a little bit.

To compress a group of images and then send the images via e-mail, follow these steps:

    ① Select the images to send, and right-click any one of them in the group.

    ② Click Send To, and then click Compressed (Zipped) Folder.

    ③ Name the folder when prompted. The folder will appear with a zipper on it.

    ④ Right-click the folder, click Send To, and then click E-Mail Recipient.

## Burn Pictures to a CD

Another way to share your pictures is to burn them to a CD. It's easy to pass around a CD and to mail it to someone who isn't computer savvy (regarding opening and saving e-mail attachments, anyway, such as your grandmother). Burning and sharing a CD is also a good way to share an entire collection of photos without taking the time to e-mail them in small groups or put them on a Web site.

You can burn a CD in two ways: You can insert a blank CD and use Windows, or you can use Windows Photo Gallery.

### USING THE WINDOWS VISTA BUILT-IN CD-BURNING FEATURE

 **10 minutes**

To burn images to a CD by using the built-in CD-burning feature in Windows Vista, follow these steps:

    ① Insert a blank writable CD in the CD drive.

    ② When prompted, click Burn Files To Disc Using Windows.

③ Type a name for the CD, and click Next.

④ Open the Pictures folder, and drag the pictures to burn to the CD window, as shown in Figure 4-2.

The files burn automatically to the CD.

⑤ When you've added all the images you want, eject the CD from the CD drive. Depending on the disc you've selected, a CD+R or CD+RW for instance, Windows Vista may prompt you to wait a few minutes while it completes the burning tasks prior to ejecting.

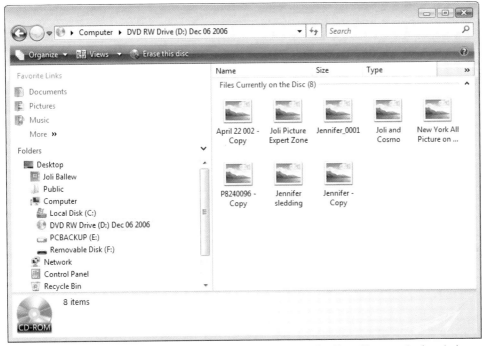

Figure 4-2: To add files to the CD drive's window, drag and drop. The files will appear in the window once dropped there.

## BURN A CD BY USING WINDOWS PHOTO GALLERY

**15 minutes**

Another way to burn a CD of images is using Windows Photo Gallery. A Burn tab offers options to burn a data disc or a video DVD. We'll talk about DVDs later; for now, we'll focus just on putting pictures on a CD.

To burn a CD by using Windows Photo Gallery, follow these steps:

1. Open Windows Photo Gallery from the Start menu. If it isn't there already, type **Windows Photo Gallery** in the Start Search box, and then click its name when it appears.

2. Select the images to burn. Note that you can select entire folders, the entire library, or certain folders or images. Just hold down the Ctrl key while selecting, as shown in Figure 4-3.

3. Once you've selected all the images, click Burn, Data Disc, also as shown in Figure 4-3.

Figure 4-3: To start a CD-burning project, click Burn, Data Disc.

④ Depending on your drive and media, you may be prompted to prepare the CD. If prompted, type a title for the CD, and choose a file system from the following two options. If you want to share the CD with others who can watch it on their own CD/DVD player, choose the second option.

**Live File System**   Lets you add and erase files from the CD, but the CD may not be readable on operating systems prior to Windows XP.

**Mastered**   Readable on all computers and newer CD/DVD players. Once files are written to the disc, they cannot be erased.

⑤ In the CD/DVD window, verify the data you want is listed, and click Burn To Disc. If prompted again, name the disc, and select a burn speed. Click Next.

# Create a **DVD of Pictures and Watch It on a TV**

**25 minutes to a couple of hours**

Did you know you can create a DVD by using your own DVD recorder and Windows DVD Maker in Windows Vista and then pass it along to someone who can then watch it on their TV by using their own DVD player? You can, and this feature is totally awesome. What's better than sharing, though, is that you can create a DVD you can watch on your *own* DVD player whenever you want! All you need is Windows DVD Maker (which comes with Windows Vista), a writable DVD, and a DVD recorder. Not only can you burn a DVD to watch on a TV, but you can also create professional-looking menus with your choice of font and font characteristics, a scene selection page, and slide shows of your pictures. To get started, pop in a blank DVD, and wait for the prompt shown in Figure 4-4. Click Burn A DVD Video Disc, and Windows DVD Maker will open.

**Figure 4-4:** To start a Windows DVD Maker project, click Burn A DVD Video Disc.

## ADD PICTURES TO A BLANK DVD

With Windows DVD Maker open, follow these steps:

1. Click Add Items.

2. In the Add Items To Add window, browse to the files to add, select them, and click Add. (Notice as you add pictures, Windows Vista creates a slide show automatically.)

3. Repeat steps 1 and 2 to add pictures until you have added what you want to add or until you've used up all the available minutes on the DVD. In Figure 4-5, you can see that we have used only 2 of the available 150 minutes so far.

4. Type a disc title in the Disc Title box. (Do *not* click Next.)

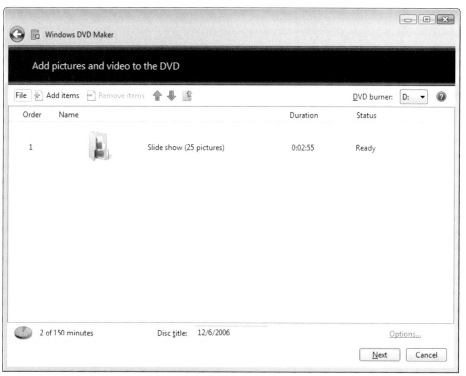

**Figure 4-5:** Add as many pictures as you like until you run out of pictures to add or until you run out of space on the DVD.

## SET OPTIONS

With the images added to the Windows DVD Maker window, set the options for your DVD by following these steps:

1.  Click Options.

2.  Select one of the following to configure how you want your DVD to play:

    • Select the radio button Start With DVD Menu if you want the DVD menu to display when the DVD is inserted in a DVD player.

    • Select the radio button Play Video And End With DVD Menu if you want the video to play immediately when the DVD is inserted and also show the menu when the video ends.

    • Select the radio button Play Video In A Continuous Loop if you want the video to play automatically and loop continuously.

3.  Select the radio button to set the DVD aspect ratio. Choose from a 16:9 (widescreen) or 4:3 (standard) aspect ratio.

4.  Select the radio button to set the video format. You have the following two choices:

    **NTSC**  The television system used by Canada, Japan, South Korea, the Phillipines, and the United States, as well as other countries, mainly in the Americas.

    **PAL**  The dominant system in other countries, including the Netherlands, New Zealand, Vietnam, Ethiopia, Fiji, Brazil, Australia, and most of Europe. Most of the time you will not need to change this setting from NTSC, unless you plan to share your DVD with a friend or family member who doesn't live in the United States or in one of the countries just listed.

5.  Select the DVD burner speed from the drop-down list of options (Fastest, Medium, Slow). The default choice for this option is Fastest. Leave this setting as is unless you have problems burning a DVD; in that case, try Medium or Slow.

6.  To change the storage location for temporary files that are created when making a DVD, click Browse, select the new folder location, and then click OK. There's almost no need to change this.

## CONFIGURE MENU OPTIONS

Click Next after adding pictures and configuring options for your DVD. You'll see the screen shown in Figure 4-6.

Once you've added all your files and chosen the burner and title, click Next. At the screen shown in Figure 4-6, follow these steps:

**1** Click Menu Text, and add any of the following:

- Click the arrow next to the Font box, and then select the font for the menu text.

- Click the Color, Bold, and Italics buttons to select the font color and formatting.

- Type a disc title.

- Type a label for the button to play the DVD.

- Type a label for the button to display the scenes on your DVD.

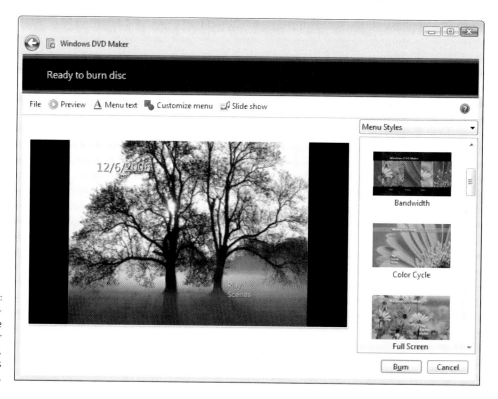

**Figure 4-6:**
After con-
figuring the
options for
your DVD,
you'll see this
screen.

- Type a label for the button to display the notes on your DVD.

- Type any notes for the DVD.

**2** Click Change Text.

## ACCESS THE CUSTOMIZE MENU

As with the menu text, you can change the menu style. You can change the font in the same manner as you did the menu text, but you can also add foreground video, background video, and menu audio. In addition, you can choose from several scene styles. If you decide to add any media items, such as foreground or background video, you'll have to click Browse and locate the media to add. Once finished, click Change Style. If you choose not to add any of these items, click Don't Change.

Here's the scoop on the foreground, background, and audio options:

- Foreground video is a video that you want to appear on the menu page when you put the DVD in a DVD player. The menu options, including Play and Scenes, are positioned on top of the selected video.

- Background video is a video that you want to appear before the menu page opens when watching the DVD on a DVD player. With a background video, the video appears and plays, and then menu options such as Play and Scenes become available.

**NOTE** When both a foreground video and a background video are selected, the background video plays first, and then the foreground video plays and offers menu options.

- A media audio file for background music plays music while the menu is displayed for your DVD.

**TIP** To see the menu as it will appear when you play your DVD, click Preview. If you don't like it, make changes before continuing.

## CHANGE SLIDE SHOW SETTINGS

To change the settings for your slide show, click the Slide Show button. On the Slide Show Settings page, change any of the following:

- Click Add Music, browse to the music file you want to add, and then click Open. Add music files if your slide show is longer than the song you selected. (You can change the order of the music added by selecting the song and then clicking the Move Up or Move Down button.)

- Verify the slide show length is a close match with the music added. If not, click Change Slide Show Length To Match Music Length.

- Note that you can also specify the duration for each picture to display in the slide show by selecting an option from the Picture Length option drop-down list.

- Select a transition for the slides in the Transition Choices drop-down list.

- Add pan and zoom effects to the pictures you include in your slide show, if desired, by clicking Use Pan And Zoom Effects For Pictures.

Click Change Slide Show to complete the transition. Figure 4-7 shows an example.

**Figure 4-7:** Decide what the slide show should look like in its final form.

## SELECT A STYLE AND BURN THE DVD

To finish, select a menu style from the Windows DVD Maker choices, and click Burn. Figure 4-8 shows one choice, Reflections, and reminds us of the new Flip 3D inter-face in Windows Vista.

**Figure 4-8:** Click Burn to burn the DVD.

# Get Your Photos Printed from an Online Photo Store

Sometimes you just want to see your pictures on the printed page. Sure, you can print them by using your own printer at home, but somehow, that just doesn't cut it. No matter what paper you use, what settings, or how you configure the printer, profes-sional print shops almost always produce better results. It's not just that, though; it's cheaper too. By the time you purchase the ink and paper, buy the printer, and print your images, you've spent more than just sending your pictures off to the print store!

You have a lot of options for getting real prints. You can take your memory card or CD of pictures to a neighborhood store and let them do it, or you can get your pictures printed online. We're all about not leaving the house, so we'll walk you through ordering some prints online.

## SET YOUR OPTIONS

You have a ton of options when choosing an online store to print your photos, including Shutterfly (*www.shutterfly.com*), Kodak EasyShare Gallery (*www.kodakgallery.com*), Snapfish (*www.snapfish.com*), Bonusprint (*www.bonusprint.com*), and hundreds of others. Although it may be difficult to know which one to choose, we suggest one of these four.

You should expect to pay no more than $.12 US to $.15 US per print, you should get your initial 25 or so prints free (or some equivalent bonus) for signing up, and you should be able to share your prints online for free. You should also look for editing options, with at least the options to enhance the color, change the tint, and crop photos before sending them to the printer.

**TIP** You can order prints directly from Windows Photo Gallery too. Just click Print, and click Order Prints.

## WALK-THROUGH: PURCHASE A PHOTO PRINT ONLINE

To obtain prints from an online source, you generally need to first register and then upload and edit your prints. Once you've done that, you can then decide how many copies you want to print of each and decide whether you'd like to put them on the Web for others to view.

To register, upload, and obtain prints from an online photo-printing company, in general you'll follow these steps:

1. Go to the site, perhaps *www.shutterfly.com*.
2. Click Get Started (or Register), and create a user name and password.
3. Click Add Pictures, and when prompted, create an album name.

④ Install any upload assistants or software required by the company.

⑤ Browse to the location of the files on your hard drive, and select the check boxes of the ones you want to upload. Start the upload process.

⑥ When the upload completes, click View Pictures or Continue.

⑦ Order copies of the images you've uploaded.

The rest of the process depends on what you decide to order. However, you can generally choose from different sizes, quantities, and finishes. You can also double-click each image to crop it or perform additional editing as the site allows.

In this chapter, you learned how to share your pictures in even more ways. From e-mailing photos to burning CDs to creating slide shows on DVDs to ordering prints online, you can share your pictures with others in a ton of ways!

- Create a photo diary

- Use your pictures as a screen-saver slide show

- Create the perfect gift by using your own photos

- Create an online picture blog with Windows Live Spaces

# **Get** Creative with Photos

# CHAPTER 5

You can get really creative with your pictures if you put your mind to it. For instance, you can create and keep a photo diary, one you'll enjoy yourself now and your kids will treasure later. Just take a few pictures every week or every month, and organize them in a library. Add a few comments to each image, and in no time you will have created a priceless journal of your life.

You can also create gifts from photos. With myriad options online, you can put pictures on T-shirts, coffee mugs, and more. You can create your own greeting cards too, as well as create an online library of your favorite photos. Finally, you can create a slide show for an event, such as a class reunion or a friend's 30th birthday, simply by creating a screen saver for your PC! And that is just the beginning.

# Create a Photo Journal/Diary

*You can get really creative with your pictures if you put your mind to it.*

This is our absolute favorite way to share and use our photos. It's also a wonderful way to document your life, your kids' lives, and your relatives' most important events. You can take this project as far as you'd like; you can start with something as simple as taking pictures of everyday events, uploading them to your PC, and adding comments to them in Windows Photo Gallery; or you can create a monthly slide show of your images, complete with themes, transitions, and title pages by using Windows DVD Maker (like you learned in the previous chapter), and then burn the show to a DVD.

## TAKE PICTURES OF EVERYDAY EVENTS

 15 minutes

If you've ever kept a diary or journal, you know how much fun it is to read it years later. Even the most mundane topics are awesome, such as reminiscing about the crush you had on the quarterback of your high school's football team or getting your first apartment or car. That being said, you'll want to get started with your video diary by taking pictures of everyday events, such as dropping your kids off at school and cooking dinner, and by taking pictures of special events, such as going to a concert or visiting an old friend.

Here are some more ideas for pictures to include in your digital journal:

**Your kids and their friends playing**   It's amazing how fast they grow up!

**Your spouse and friends at backyard get-togethers**   It's amazing how fast they get old!

**Reunions, weddings, birthday parties, graduations, and other special events**   It's always fun to look back at these events, and you can create DVDs to share with participants and attendees. You can bet they'll cherish them forever.

**Raking and jumping in leaves in the fall, shoveling snow and creating snowmen in the winter, waterskiing and boating in the summer**  Ah, these are memories of those wonderful carefree days; it's always fun to look back.

**New houses, new cars, new pets, new boats, and the like**  You can document these subjects for insurance purposes, to remember them as puppies and kittens, and to relive how you felt the day you acquired them.

**New technologies**  Do this so you can look back and say, "Remember when we used to have to parallel park the car ourselves?" or "Remember the first computer we had that had a whopping 1GB hard drive?"

## CREATE A JOURNAL FOLDER AND ADD PICTURES

**15 to 45 minutes**

To get started, you'll want to create a folder just for your journal entries. We suggest creating a subfolder in the Pictures folder named Journal, with subfolders for each week's or month's entries. Figure 5-1 shows an example.

**Figure 5-1:** When first starting a picture journal, create folders and subfolders that will help you stay organized.

With this system, a folder named Journal 2007 holds 12 subfolders, each for one month of the year. Inside each subfolder are the uploaded images for that month. When uploading the images, all you have to do to stay organized is to browse to the appropriate subfolder and name the uploaded images with the date they were taken. This system makes it easy to upload files to the correct folder, makes it simple to find them, and makes it simple to back up the images to DVD (just drag the entire Journal folder to a writable DVD window).

> **TIP** Once you've taken pictures of the week's events and uploaded them to your PC, make sure you delete them from your camera. This will help you keep your pictures organized in their proper folders and avoid duplicates from popping up in the wrong ones. (If you're not quite up to keeping a weekly journal, then take pictures for the month, and designate a day each month to catch up on your journal.)

## USE WINDOWS PHOTO GALLERY AND ADD COMMENTS TO PICTURES

 **5 minutes**

With the pictures on your PC and in the correct folder, you can now add the folder to Windows Photo Gallery, open the folder to access the pictures, and add personal notes, just as you would with any journal or diary. The only difference here is, you're adding comments to a picture.

Before you can add comments in Windows Photo Gallery, though, you have to tell it that you want access to that folder. To add the Journal folder to Windows Photo Gallery, follow these steps:

1. Open Windows Photo Gallery.

2. Click File, Add Folder To Gallery. (You're going to add your new Journal folder and subfolders.)

3. In the Add Folders To Gallery dialog box, click the triangle next to your user name, click the triangle next to Pictures, and then click the Journal folder you recently created, as shown in Figure 5-2. (If you created the Journal folder somewhere else, browse to it.) Click OK.

4. You can now access this folder inside Windows Photo Gallery.

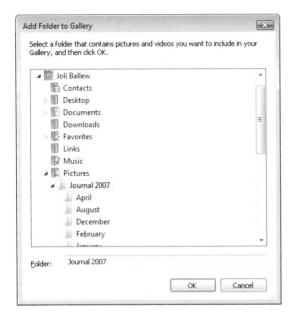

Figure 5-2: You can add any folder to Windows Photo Gallery.

Now you can add comments. To add comments to images in your Journal folder by using Windows Photo Gallery, follow these steps:

1. In Windows Photo Gallery, locate the image to which you want to add notes and comments.

2. Right-click the image, and click Add Tags. In the right pane, the Info pane, create a tag for the picture if it does not already have one. You can use the tags to sort the pictures later.

3. Click Add Caption. Add a caption that describes the picture. When you add a caption, the caption can display during a slide show if you like.

4. Right-click the picture again, and this time click Properties. (Note that you can select multiple pictures too.) The image's Properties dialog box appears.

5. On the Details tab, click Title to add a title, click Subject to add a subject, and click Comments to add a comment, among other options. When you click one of the items, you have to start typing to see the dialog box—when you click, it just looks like you have selected it. It's there, though, as shown in Figure 5-3.

6. Click OK to save the changes.

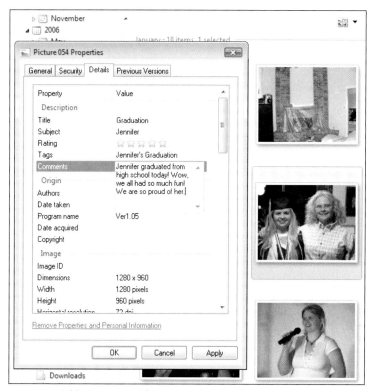

**Figure 5-3:** Add comments, titles, tags, ratings, and more in the Properties dialog box of any picture.

With pictures in your library and with tags, comments, titles, ratings, and the like, you can now sort and view images in a lot more ways than before. Go ahead, take a look. Click each folder in Windows Photo Gallery once. You'll not only see the images in your Journal folder and subfolders that you just uploaded but you'll also see the images appear elsewhere too. That's because a lot of folders already created have set criteria that match the images you've uploaded.

As an example, in our January 2007 folder, we have 10 items. However, those items also appear in the Recently Imported folder, in several folders under Tags, in the January 2007 Date Taken folders, and in folders based on ratings.

# Create a Screen-Saver Slide Show

 **5 to 15 minutes**

In the previous chapter you learned how to create awesome slide shows to burn to a DVD by using Windows DVD Maker. However, you don't have to be that fancy about it or put that much work into it. You can create a screen-saver slide show from the pictures you've taken and uploaded to your PC in only a few minutes. And you don't have to settle for just any old show either. You can set criteria for the slide show based on many attributes. For instance, you can create a slide-show screen saver that contains only images that

- are tagged (or not tagged) with a specific word or words,

- have a specific rating or higher or have no rating at all,

- are from a particular folder, or

- apply a theme to your screen saver if your video card supports it.

You can also change the slide show speed from slow to medium or fast, and you can shuffle the contents of the slide show. Here's how:

1. Open Windows Photo Gallery.

2. Click the File menu, and then click Screen Saver Settings.

3. Under Screen Saver, select Photos in the leftmost list, as shown in Figure 5-4.

4. Click Settings. You can configure two options: The Use All Pictures And Videos From Photo Gallery option has these settings:

   - With This Tag (type the tag you want to match to)

   - With This Rating Or Higher (select the appropriate rating)

   - Don't Show Items Tagged (type the tag you want to match to)

   The Use Pictures And Videos From option has these settings:

   - C:\Users\username\Pictures (the default Pictures folder)

   - Browse (any folder you want)

⑤ Select a theme and a slide show speed, and select Shuffle Contents if desired, from their respective drop-down lists.

⑥ Configure how long to wait for the screen saver to be applied. Click OK.

This makes a perfect backdrop for a party at your home. You can show pictures of an event, of a vacation, or even of the guests at the party. For the latter, create a folder named Party, and add images to it as the party progresses. Let the screen saver come on after a minute of inactivity (activity being you adding more pictures), and change the slide show all night long!

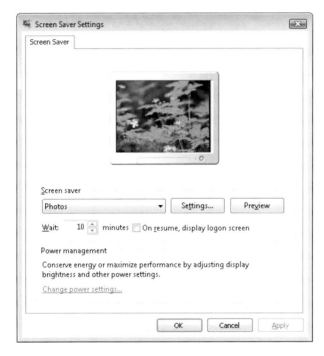

Figure 5-4: You can create a slide show for a screen saver and enjoy your pictures all the time.

**TIP** Although you could use Windows DVD Maker to create a slide show complete with transitions, themes, and other effects, if you just need a quick slide show for an event, such as a birthday party, put all the pictures that relate to it in a single folder, and from Windows Photo Gallery, configure a slide show to show only the pictures in that folder. Just set the screen-saver settings so that the screen show is always on, and you're good to go.

# CREATE THE PERFECT GIFT ONLINE

Although creating a gift from a photo isn't exactly related to the Windows Vista operating system, it is a nice aside when you're trying to find that perfect present. You can put a photo on just about anything, from a calendar to a T-shirt to a coffee mug. At *www.imagestation.com*, for instance, you can put your favorite pictures on photo books, bags, mugs, totes, calendars, greeting cards, confections, T-shirts, mousepads, puzzles, and more. If you can't figure out what to get the birthday boy, a puzzle with his picture on it may just be the ticket!

# Create a Web Photo Blog

You can upload photos to a ton of places on the Web, and once uploaded, you can then share the images with the people of your choosing. Maybe you'd like to share pictures of your family with relatives who live thousands of miles away but everyone is getting tired of e-mailing or burning and sending DVDs. Perhaps you need to keep up-to-date pictures of a project you're working on, or you want to create and publish a daily blog of your adventures.

Whatever the case, Microsoft offers a place to do that, called Windows Live Spaces, and by using it, you can get started sharing your photos online extremely quickly. With Windows Live Spaces you can upload your favorite photos to your *space* and then create a blog about them, all for free. (*Blog* is short for *Weblog*, which is an online diary of sorts.) With Windows Live Spaces, there's no limit to what you can share or with whom!

## CREATE YOUR WINDOWS LIVE SPACE

 **15 to 30 minutes**

If you don't yet have a space at Windows Live Spaces, now is the time to get one. Go to *http://spaces.live.com/* to get started, and then follow these steps:

1. Click Create Your Space.

2. Type a MSN Hotmail, MSN Messenger, or Passport account name to log in. If you don't have one of those either, click Sign Up For Windows Live, and get one.

③ Once logged in, type a name for your new space to be associated with your Windows Live Spaces Web address. Figure 5-5 shows how we configured ours.

④ Click Check Availability. If the name is already in use, type another until you find one that isn't.

⑤ Click Create to create your space.

> **NOTE** If you'd like to take some time now to create a profile, invite friends, or further refine the site before continuing, feel free to spend as much time doing that as you'd like!

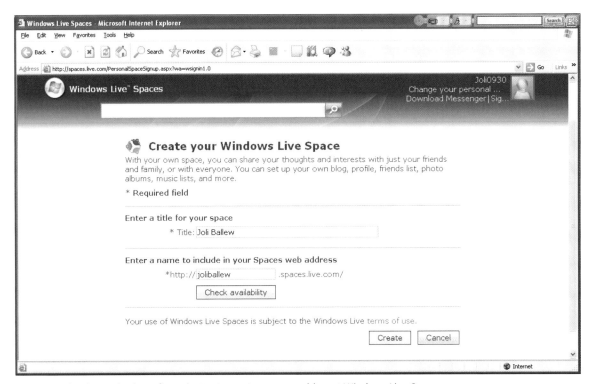

Figure 5-5: It takes only about five minutes to create your own blog at Windows Live Spaces.

## PUT YOUR FAVORITE PICTURES ON YOUR SPACE

5 to 30 minutes

Once you've created your space, you can add pictures and more to it. Figure 5-6 shows what your space might look like when you first create it. As you can see here, there aren't any pictures yet, there are no friends, there's no book list, and, well, it's a little empty. Let's post some pictures first.

To add pictures to your Windows Live Spaces space, follow these steps:

1  Under Photos, click Add. You can see the Photos category on the top-right side in Figure 5-6. It's just above Updated Spaces, Archives, and Book List.

2  Click Add Photos. (If prompted by a yellow bar at the top of Windows Internet Explorer 7 in Windows Vista, click it, click Install ActiveX Control, and click Add Photos again.)

3  If prompted, click Install to install the Windows Live Photo Upload control. You must install this control to upload pictures. This tool lets you preview pictures on your computer and select multiple photos to upload.

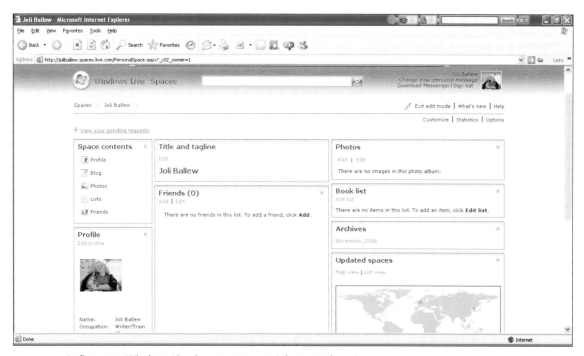

Figure 5-6: At first, your Windows Live Spaces space won't have much on it.

④ Browse to the location on your PC where the pictures are. Select them, and click Open to add them to the upload page.

⑤ When finished selecting photos, click Upload.

⑥ Click Save And Close.

You'll now see a slide show of the images you uploaded right on your Windows Live Spaces space. You can add albums, change the picture titles, and more, all by clicking Edit and making the changes you desire.

## CREATE A BLOG

Along with adding photos to your Windows Live Spaces space, you can also create your own blog. Just click the Blog button on the left side of the Windows Live Spaces interface, and click Add to create a blog entry. By using the blog feature, you can write notes about the pictures you've added, including when they were taken and posted and what they represent. This is a great way to keep in touch with friends and relatives far away.

> **TIP** Explore What's New. You'll quickly find out whether your MSN contacts have blogs at Windows Live Spaces, and you can visit their spaces.

If you think about it some more, you'll probably come up with a ton of ideas for sharing your photos. However you do it, just do it! Mail a few photos, burn a couple of CDs, create a screen-saver slide show, and get yourself a space at Windows Live Spaces. It'll be fun!

# PART III  Music

- **Rip CDs to your PC**

- **Update your music library data automatically by using the Internet**

- **Change a song's properties manually including the playback speed, title, genre, and other characteristics**

- **Create different types of playlists**

- **Enhance playback**

- **Work with the new grouping options in Windows Vista**

# **Create** the Ultimate Music Library

# CHAPTER 6

The Windows Vista operating system comes well equipped with everything you need to enjoy music on your PC. If you have a powerful enough computer and the hardware to match, you can get rid of just about everything else you own for managing your music. With Windows Media Player 11, you can rip your CD library to your PC, download information automatically from the Internet, tweak songs by changing the speed at which they play, add to their metadata, and manage your media with new groupings. You can even use Windows Vista to help you optimize media playback!

Just as you did with your photos and videos, here you'll learn how to create the perfect music library and portal. By the time you're finished with this chapter and the next, you'll have your music under your complete control!

# Rip CDs to Your Media Library

*If you have a powerful enough computer and the hardware to match, you can get rid of just about everything else you own for managing your music.*

*Ripping* is the process of copying audio CDs to your PC. The first step in creating a music library is to gather your favorite CDs and put them on your PC. Look under the couch, under the backseat of the car, in your kids' rooms, in your friends' houses, in and under the CD/DVD player, and behind the stereo speakers. Once you have all your favorite CDs in a pile, make sure you haven't collected any that you really don't like. Keep in mind that although your PC may be able to hold as many CDs as you want, having a library that's larger than your portable music device will cause you to have to sync that device manually (since Windows Vista won't know what you do and don't want on it). In addition, when you play and shuffle the songs in your library, you'll have to sit through songs you don't want to hear when it's their turn to play. There's no point in dealing with music you don't really like!

### CONFIGURE MEDIA PLAYER 11 FOR OPTIMAL RIPPING

 **5 to 10 minutes**

Before you pop in that first CD to burn, you should take a few minutes to configure Media Player 11 for optimal ripping. You'll want to turn on automatic ripping when a CD is inserted, turn on automatic ejection when the rip is complete, and select the desired music file format:

1. Click Start, and in the Start Search box, type **Media Player**.

2. In the Programs list results, click Windows Media Player.

3. Click the arrow on the Rip tab, point to Rip CD Automatically When Inserted, and click Always. (You can change that after you've ripped your entire library.)

4. Click the arrow on the Rip tab again, and click Eject CD After Ripping. (Click the arrow again to verify there is a check mark next to that option, showing it's turned on.)

5. Click the arrow on the Rip tab again, and click More Options.

**⑥** In the Options dialog box that appears, shown in Figure 6-1, verify Format is set to Windows Media Audio. As you can see in Figure 6-1, this creates an Audio Quality setting of 128 kilobits per second (Kbps), the default audio quality, and each CD will take approximately 56MB of disk space on the computer. (If you'd like to see how other formats compare, click Compare Formats Online.)

**⑦** Verify Copy Protect Music is not selected. You can always select it later if you like. Read the sidebar "About Copy Protection" later in this chapter to help you decide. Click OK.

> **TIP** Connect to the Internet while ripping your CD library, and Media Player will automatically (by default) locate and update the media information on your PC. This includes album art, album title, track numbers and titles, and more. If you do not connect to the Internet, you may not see any information at all regarding the CDs you've ripped.

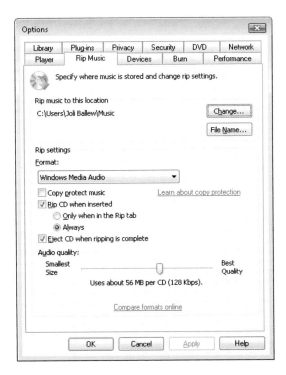

**Figure 6-1:** The Options dialog box, specifically the Rip Music tab, lets you see your current rip settings and configure the format of the songs you rip.

# ABOUT COPY **PROTECTION**

In the previous section you encountered a setting for copy protecting your music. We suggested you *not* select that particular setting just yet. However, sometimes it may be in your best interest to do so. To find out whether you should select Copy Protect Music on the Rip Music tab in the Options dialog box, you'll want to understand what copy protection is.

When you choose to copy protect a file, it means you want to require whoever accesses the file to have certain rights to play it, burn it to a DVD, or sync it to a portable device. When this is selected, even if *you* copy the files to another computer and try to use them, you'll be prompted to download the rights for the file before you can use it. You can download these rights only a limited number of times. So if you plan to rip your CDs to multiple computers, we suggest you do not select this option. If you want to limit how many times a person can copy or distribute a file you've ripped, select it. You might want to do this if you've created your own music!

Also, understand that you cannot remove copy protection from a file once you've turned it on.

To fill you in on some background, copy protection came about as a way for content providers, such as online music stores and producers of publicly distributed CDs, to assign particular rights to you based on how you acquired the media. If you purchase a CD, for example, you have more rights than if you subscribe to the media online. If you own the music, you own it, and for the most part you can do whatever you like with it (to a point). If you're just renting the music, you can generally use it for playing on one PC, burning to one CD, and syncing to a portable device.

If all of this talk about subscriptions to online music services seems odd to you, no worries—you'll learn much more about online media later!

## RIP CDS

**2 to 5 minutes per CD**

To rip a CD with the settings configured properly as detailed in the previous section, simply open Media Player 11, put the CD in the CD drive, and wait while the CD rips. (If you'd like to watch the progress of the rip, click Ripping CD at the bottom of the player's interface.) When the CD has been ripped, it will eject automatically. Put in another CD, and repeat this process until your entire CD collection is on your PC.

Now, this is an incredible feat for some people; if you have 1,000 CDs, for instance, it may take you a while to get all your music on your PC. However, once it's done, you're going to absolutely love it. And other than taking a bit of time, it's extremely easy to do.

# Change Default Settings for Additional Privacy

If you were connected to the Internet when you ripped your CD library, you probably noticed that even when ripping your oldest CDs, Media Player was able to retrieve the album name, album art, year, genre, track numbers and titles, and more. That's because, by default, Media Player is configured to retrieve additional information about ripped music from the Internet and add any missing information it finds. And it can almost always find something about the CD you're ripping! In addition to obtaining this type of information automatically, Media Player also looks for updates to the player, downloads *codecs* (data needed to play certain media files), and downloads media usage rights.

Now, all of this is just fine with us. We're shocked when Media Player can locate the track names for an old Rainbow album or a waltz from way back. However, if you'd rather not have Media Player obtain this information automatically or if you'd like to change the defaults from, say, adding only missing information rather than over-writing all the media information with what it finds, you certainly can. As with other configuration changes, you achieve this through the Options dialog box.

To make changes to the default settings of Media Player for obtaining media information on the Internet, click the arrow on any tab in Media Player, and then click

More Options. From there, work through the tabs in the Options dialog box to configure the settings as you'd like. Here are some tabs you may want to consider initially:

**Player**   Change whether and how often (once a day, once a week, once a month) Media Player should look for updates.

**Privacy**   Change whether media information retrieved from the Internet should be displayed or whether that information should be retrieved at all. The player can also look for media usage licenses when you play a file and look to see whether these rights should be refreshed. Finally, you can decide not to save file and uniform resource locator (URL) history in the player, and you can clear caches for CDs, DVDs, and devices. The latter might be important if you share your computer with your kids, a co-worker, or another relative.

**Security**   Change defaults to play enhanced content from Web pages automatically, to show local captions when present, and to run script commands when present. Running scripts is a bit dangerous, and scripts can contain viruses; therefore, we suggest forgoing running them.

# **Fix** Songs **to Suit Your Preferences**

With Media Player 11 on Windows Vista you have more control than ever over your music. For example, you can slow down a song's tempo or speed it up. If you do this for multiple songs, put them in a playlist, and then sync them to a portable music device, you can create the ultimate workout playlist. Imagine, every song in your Workout playlist plays at the same speed as the rate you jog!

You can also edit the album title, artist, genre, year, and song titles. This is important when you have multiple versions of a song or when you deem the information retrieved from the Internet incorrect or incomplete. After all, how can you have the perfect music library if the information isn't right? It's possible to rate songs as well and even add your own information about the artist, type the lyrics, add pictures you've found on the Web, and include your own personal comments. Imagine, you take pictures at a concert, add them to the library, and then add comments about your experience! If you wanted, you could spend hours upon hours just tweaking your library.

## CHANGE THE SPEED OF A SONG

You can change the speed of any song by using the Play Speed settings under Enhancement on the Now Playing tab. You might want to increase how fast a song plays to make it the ultimate workout song, as mentioned earlier, or slow it down so you can learn a guitar riff (or try to figure out the words). Changing the speed does not change the key of the song as it did with record players, though, which means that slowing down a song won't make that song's key go any lower and speeding it up won't make the group sound like the Chipmunks!

To change the playback speed of any song, follow these steps:

1. In Media Player 11, click the Library tab.

2. Select a song to play.

3. Click the Now Playing tab, click Enhancements, and click Play Speed Settings.

4. Move the slider to the left to slow the song down or to the right to speed it up. You can also click Slow, Normal, or Fast, as shown in Figure 6-2.

**Figure 6-2:**
Change the playback speed of any song by moving the slider to the left or right.

## EDIT ANYTHING

You can edit just about anything in Media Player 11. To find out whether something is editable, right-click it, and look for the word *Edit*. It may be a stand-alone command, or it may appear in a menu of commands. If you see Edit, click it; the editable text will turn blue (this means it's highlighted and selected), and all you have to do is type text to replace what's there. Figure 6-3 shows an example of a stand-alone Edit option.

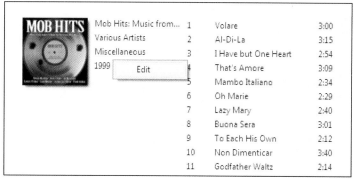

**Figure 6-3:** To see whether something is editable, right-click it, and look for the word *Edit*.

## ADD PICTURES, LYRICS, AND COMMENTS

To further complete your music library, you can add pictures, lyrics, and comments. You can achieve all this by right-clicking a song and clicking Advanced Tag Editor. You won't see the Advanced Tag Editor command when right-clicking an album cover, an album title, or the year the album was created, but you will get the option when you right-click a track (song) title, as shown in Figure 6-4.

> **TIP** To select multiple noncontiguous tracks, hold down the Ctrl key while selecting. To select contiguous tracks, hold down the Shift key while selecting.

**Figure 6-4:** The Advanced Tag Editor command lets you add metadata to a song or group of songs.

The Advanced Tag Editor dialog box contains five tabs:

**Track Info** Type the title, subtitle, track number, beats per minute, album name, original album name, set, and subgenre in their respective text boxes. Select an option from the drop-down lists for genre, mood, key, and language to create advanced tag entries for each of these items. Note that if you don't see what you want in the drop-down list, you can type your own option. Figure 6-5 shows an example.

**Artist Info** Type information for artist, lyricist, album artist, original lyricist, conductor, composer, and original artist. Click Web Sites to add a URL for the artist.

**Lyrics** Type lyrics or click Synchronized Lyrics to add lyrics based on the position in the song. You can click the Help button in the Synchronized Lyrics dialog box to help you get started.

**Figure 6-5:** If you don't see what you want in any of the drop-down lists, you can type your own entry, as shown here.

**Pictures**   Click Add, and browse to the picture you want to include.

**Comments**   Type your own comments as desired.

You can add as much or as little information as you'd like. The more you add and the more precise you can be, the more exact your playlists will be. For example, if an album in your library is rated as Rock when in your mind it should be categorized as Party Tunes, you can make that change in the Advanced Tag Editor dialog box. After you've done that, when you select or create a playlist based on what you deem as party tunes, that album will be included.

In Figure 6-5, note that Party Tunes is not a default genre. You can see in the list that between Other and Polka, no Party Tunes exists. However, you can type any genre name you like and save your changes, and it will become a real, live genre!

**TIP** Rate any single song by clicking the desired star next to the song on the Library tab. To rate an entire album, right-click the album, click Rate, and click the desired rating. Right-click any genre, year, or other metadata to edit it too. Use your ratings to denote your favorite and least favorite songs or to further classify songs by the time of day you listen to them (one star in the morning, three starts at work, five stars at night) or by using similar criteria. You can also create playlists based on your ratings. Perhaps one star could be first-date music, two stars could be second-date music, and the like.

# **Create** Playlists

Playlists are at the heart of Media Player 11. Playlists can be static (never chang-ing) or dynamic (having the ability to update themselves when content changes). A dynamic playlist, also called an *autoplaylist*, is one that updates itself automati-cally each time you access it. So if you create an autoplaylist for songs acquired in the past 30 days, every time you add music, that playlist will change based on the changes in your library. Don't let any of this confuse you, though. Creating and using playlists is easy, no matter what type you choose.

A good playlist to create is an autoplaylist that contains the songs you listen to most. You can name the playlist My Favorite Songs. When creating the playlist, configure the criteria so that the 40 or so songs you listen to most in your music library are the only songs in it. As your tastes change, so will the items in the list. Another good playlist to create is a static playlist that contains only those songs related to a specific event, say a dinner party. You wouldn't want to chance shuf-fling all the songs in your music library at a dinner party, or to chance playing an older dynamic playlist, for fear of something playing that's offensive, too loud, or not music at all (such as a comedy clip).

## CREATE A STATIC PLAYLIST FOR AN EVENT

One of the easiest playlists to create is one where you select the songs manually to create a list that does not change. You may want to create these kinds of playlists for events, such as baby showers, dinner parties, pregame get-togethers, a New Year's Eve party, or something similar. When you create a playlist for an event, you never have to worry about the music! No more running for the remote when a commercial comes on the radio, changing CDs when one ends, running out of music to play, or otherwise fretting over what's playing in the background.

To create a static playlist, follow these steps:

1. In Media Player 11, click the Library tab. Verify only music is listed by clicking the arrow under Library and verifying Music is selected.

2. In the Navigation pane on the left side of the interface, right-click Playlists, and click Create Playlist. (You can do this in other ways too, but as you can see, with this option you also have access to creating an autoplaylist.)

3. In the List pane, type a name for the playlist. Make sure to name it descriptively, and then press Enter.

4. By using the pointer, work through the categories in your library, and drag the songs you want in the playlist to the List pane. You can drag entire albums or entire genres, and you can select multiple songs at a time by using the Shift or Ctrl key.

5. Once you've added all the songs you want, click Save Playlist.

The playlist appears under Playlists in the Navigation pane. You can now work with this playlist as you would any category in Media Player. You can play it, burn it, edit it, and delete it.

## CREATE AN AUTOPLAYLIST OF YOUR FAVORITE SONGS

A must-have autoplaylist is the My Favorite Songs playlist. You'll have to create it yourself, and what's in it will be unique to you and your PC. You can then play this when you don't want to mess around with the library and just want to hear your favorite tunes.

To create this autoplaylist, you'll need to set the criteria for the list to include your most-played songs:

**1** In Media Player 11, right-click Playlists, and click Create Auto Playlist.

**2** In the New Auto Playlist dialog box, as shown in Figure 6-6 with all the information for this example set, type an autoplaylist name. For this list, we suggest typing **My Favorite Songs**.

**3** Under Music In My Library, click Click Here To Add Criteria, and click Total Overall. Next is the Play Count option; set Total Overall to Is Greater Than, and type **20** (or another number of your choosing) for the times played.

**4** Under And Also Include, click Click Here To Add Criteria, and click Music In My Library.

**5** Under And Apply The Following Restrictions To The Auto Playlist, select Click Here To Add Criteria.

**6** Click either Limit Number Of Items To (to select how many songs should be in the playlist) or Limit Total Duration To (to select how long the playlist should last). Select Click To Set to type an amount of a time.

**7** Click OK.

Figure 6-6: To set criteria for an autoplaylist, select Click Here To Add Criteria, and then click the criteria to set.

# Optimize the Listening Experience

Now that you have a few playlists, you're going to want to listen to them, right? Well, don't just listen—experience! With the Enhancements pane in Media Player, you can really tweak how the music plays, sounds, and looks. Let's take a peek:

1. Open Media Player 11, and under Playlists, click a playlist you've previously created. (If you're skipping around, just play any album.)

2. Click the Now Playing tab.

3. Click the arrow on the Now Playing tab, click Enhancements, and then click Show Enhancements.

4. In the Enhancements pane, you'll see new options, which you can browse through by clicking the left and right arrows in that pane, shown in Figure 6-7. Click one of these arrow to move through the enhancements.

**Figure 6-7:** Enhancements include a graphic equalizer, quiet mode, Sequence Retrieval System (SRS) WOW effects, and more, all to enhance your listening and viewing experience. Click the arrows to move from one enhancement to the next.

The enhancements you can use to improve your listening experience include the following:

**Quiet mode**  Turn on quiet mode to make the difference in loud and soft sounds a medium difference or a little difference. This is most useful for watching DVDs, when the sounds of some scenes are too quiet while the sounds of others are too loud.

**SRS WOW effects**  Turn on these effects to add TruBass and WOW effect settings to enhance how music sounds. This is best used when you have high-end speakers for your PC.

**Graphic equalizer**  Turn on the graphic equalizer to configure settings for each available level or to select from a variety of preset levels such as Rock, Rap, Jazz, Folk, and more.

**Cross-fading** Turn on cross-fading to create a smooth transition between songs by fading out the song that's playing and fading in the song that's up next.

**Volume leveling** Turn on volume leveling to keep loud and soft sounds at about the safe level. This is great for live albums where the volume goes from loud to soft often and causes listening distractions.

Media Player offers other settings, but for now, these are the ones in which you may be most interested. We'll get to more of the others later.

# Group Music in Various Ways

When you can group your media so that it's accessible faster and more organized than ever, you're making life easier on yourself and anyone else who accesses your media. Media Player 11 offers two new features to help you do just that: stacking and WordWheel. Most likely, you've seen these groupings in Media Player but weren't quite sure what they were. Perhaps you've seen representations of your media that looked like stacks of albums, or maybe you've had a flashback of the local club's Internet jukebox while browsing your own media. We'll go ahead and define the terms, just so we can say we did.

## STACKING

Figure 6-8 shows *stacking*, which is a visual representation of how much media is included in a specific category, in this case Genre. In this example, the New Age genre has only a couple of albums, but the Rock genre has many. To see this visual stack, you need to have more than one item in a category. If you haven't seen any stacks yet, in the Navigation pane, click Genre and then Year. If you're going to see stacks, you'll probably see them in one of these categories. Additionally, you can add more music to your library by ripping more of your CDs, and build stacks that way.

**Figure 6-8:** Stacking offers a visual representation of how much music is in a specific category of your music library.

## WORDWHEEL

WordWheel is a feature in Media Player 11 that lets you scroll through your library by using the scroll wheel on your wheel mouse. Just like an expensive Internet jukebox, you can scroll though thousands of albums in only a few seconds. You can see the WordWheel feature by viewing the media in your library alphabetically. One way to do this is to click Artist, Contributing Artist, or something similar, in the Navigation pane. Figure 6-9 shows the Contributing Artist list; they are grouped alphabetically and can be scrolled through easily.

A party is a great place to get WordWheel going. Just as with a jukebox, party-goers can scroll through the songs, choose what they like, and thus control the mood of the party. (Of course, you have to trust them with your stuff, but, hey, that's your call!)

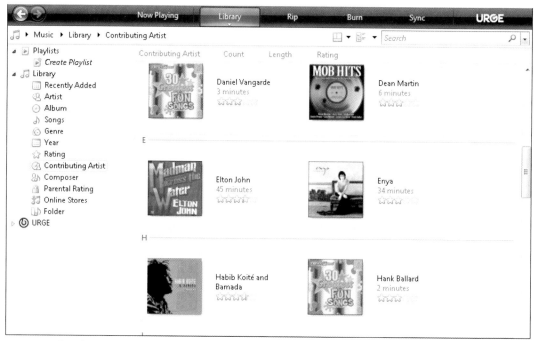

**Figure 6-9:** By using WordWheel technology, you can scroll through thousands of songs and albums instantly.

In this chapter, you learned a lot about Media Player 11, specifically how to create a tremendous music library. You learned how to rip CDs; update your music's meta-data online; change a song's title, speed, and other characteristics; create playlists, both auto and static; and group music in various ways. With that knowledge, you can now focus on experiencing your music!

- Subscribe and listen to online media
- Burn CDs for music on the go
- Select and sync a portable music device
- Stream music through your home
- Get the most from high-end speakers

# **Experience** More Music

# CHAPTER 7

You can do a lot more with Windows Media Player 11 than store, organize, and access your music. And, you can do a lot more with your music than listening to it by using Media Player 11. You don't need to be strapped down to your PC when you have places to go and people to see!

In this chapter, we'll show you how to experience your music in many more ways than just from your PC, including how to subscribe to online media, burn CDs and include cross-fading and volume leveling, sync mobile devices, stream music through your home, and more.

# Subscribe to Online Media

*You don't need to be strapped down to your PC when you have places to go and people to see!*

The days of buying a CD at the mall are all but over. So is buying an entire CD because you really like one song on it. And soon enough, you won't even buy the music you want; you'll simply subscribe to it. By paying a monthly fee instead of purchasing CDs, your library can change as often as your tastes do, with no added expense.

## UNDERSTAND WHAT URGE IS

Subscription music services are popping up everywhere. URGE is one of them. We think URGE is the best because it offers three ways to subscribe, millions of songs to choose from, and a great variety of music genres. You can also access URGE directly from Windows Media Player 11 and Windows Media Center, which makes accessing your music easier than ever. In fact, with Media Player 11, the music you subscribe to online looks and acts just like the music you own!

Three subscription services are available from URGE. Understanding these service options will help you further understand the online subscription process and what's available to you. The three options are as follows:

**URGE All Access To Go**   Access to millions of songs, the ability to transfer songs to portable devices and burn to CDs; access to 500 playlists; access to more than 130 Internet radio stations; access to URGE feeds (music delivered straight to your PC and portable device); and access to features, interviews, and blogs from artists from around the world. It's about $15 US a month.

**URGE All Access**   Everything URGE All Access To Go is, except you don't get the ability to transfer the songs to a portable player or burn the songs to a CD. It's about $10 US a month.

**URGE By The Track**   No subscription service to music but the ability to purchase songs for about $1 US a track. Also, you get access to 20 Internet radio stations; can sample hundreds of playlists; and can access features, blogs, and interviews by music artists around the world.

## SUBSCRIBE

**15 minutes**

You can subscribe to several online media stores from Media Player 11, and since many of these stores offer a free trial, you can try them before committing to one in particular. As noted, we prefer URGE, so in this section, you'll learn how to subscribe to that service. However, if you choose another service, the process is basically the same.

To subscribe to URGE, follow these steps:

1. Rest the pointer on the URGE button in Media Player 11, and when the arrow appears, click it once to see the subscription options. Select Browse All Online Stores.

2. From the available options, click URGE.

3. Click Try It Free For 14 Days, and when prompted, click Start Free Trial. Note that with a free trial, you won't be able to burn the music you download to a CD or put it on a portable music device.

4. Type the information required to create your account. No credit card is required.

5. Click Get Started.

## DOWNLOAD MEDIA

To access the millions of songs available from URGE, simply click the URGE icon located in Media Player 11 after signing up. If you're connected to the Internet, you'll immediately have access to all the music available. Figure 7-1 shows the icon.

**Figure 7-1:** Once you start your free subscription or subscribe to URGE, you'll have access to the media from Media Player 11.

With your subscription, you can listen to music all day and all night, without ever actually downloading the music to your PC. If you want to sync the music with your portable device or have the music on your hard drive so you can listen to it when you're not connected to the Internet, you'll need to download it.

To locate and download a song, multiple songs, an entire album, or a playlist of songs, browse through the URGE options to find the song, album, or playlist you want, click it, and then click Download; alternatively, right-click the song, album, or playlist to download, and click Download. That's it! Once you've downloaded a song, for example, it'll be in your library, most easily found in the Recently Added playlist. Of course, it'll also be accessible from the Artists option in the Library, and under Album, Genre, and other categories.

> **NOTE** The Search window in Media Player 11 also lets you search URGE for songs you want. Just click the URGE icon, and type what you're looking for in the Search window.

# Burn CDs for Your Car or Home

Media Player 11 offers an Audio CD option on the Burn tab. You'll use this to burn a CD of songs you like, which you can then listen to in your car or home-stereo CD player. Media Player 11 also offers two options for making those CDs better, cross-fading and autovolume leveling.

### EMPLOY CROSS-FADING AND AUTOVOLUME LEVELING

*Cross-fading*, as mentioned in Chapter 6, is having the song that's playing fade out while the song next in line fades in. This gives your music, whether on your PC, a portable device, or a CD, sound more like a radio station than a simple list of songs. *Autovolume leveling*, also introduced in Chapter 6, is another enhancement. It evens out the sounds when music comes from various sources and is of different volumes.

Autovolume leveling makes songs play at the same volume so that a song down-loaded from the Internet plays at the same volume as a song acquired from a CD. By turning on autovolume leveling, you can even out these volume changes.

To turn on these enhancements, follow these steps:

1. Click the arrow on the Now Playing tab, click Enhancements, and click Show Enhancements if it isn't already selected.

2. Click the right or left arrows in the Enhancement pane until you locate Crossfading and Auto Volume Leveling.

3. Click Turn On Auto Volume Leveling and Turn On Crossfading, as desired.

## BURN AN AUDIO CD

 **10 minutes**

You can play an audio CD in your car, your friends' cars, and any CD player in any stereo system. You'll need to have the proper ownership rights to create one, but if you do, it's quite simple to create a CD for on-the-go music.

To burn and audio CD, follow these steps:

1. In Media Player 11, click the Burn tab.

2. Browse your library, locate songs you want to put on the CD, and once located, drag them to the Burn list in the right pane. If the song has a small *i* by it, you won't be able to burn the song until you have the required license. This generally requires you to subscribe with an All Access To Go service.

3. Note that as you add songs, you can see how much time you have left on the media, in this case a blank CD. Continue to add songs as desired. If the music you want to burn spans more than a single CD, Media Player 11 can handle that. In other words, Media Player 11 can "span" multiple CDs.

4. If desired, drag songs in the order you want them to play on the CD.

5. Once you've added the music you want, click Start Burn. Figure 7-2 shows this and more.

**Figure 7-2:** Media Player 11 keeps track of how much space is left on the CD, lets you change the order of songs by dragging and dropping, shows a small *i* when a song can't be burned to a CD, and offers a Start Burn button when you're ready to burn the CD.

# Select and Sync Mobile Devices

If you listen to music on your PC, you likely also have a Zune or other portable music player that lets you take your music with you. Keeping your PC, specifically what's in Media Player 11, synced with the device is thus an important task. It's also a quite common task for you as a music lover, because you're continually download-ing new music to your PC or your portable music player, deleting music, and ripping new CDs to your library on your PC; therefore, you need to keep both libraries in sync. The Windows Vista operating system helps you do that with Media Player 11 and its sync options.

## CONNECT A MOBILE DEVICE

 **10 minutes**

First things first, though. You have to connect your mobile device! With Windows Vista, that's easy enough. Almost all the time—and 100 percent of the time if you purchase a PlaysForSure device—Media Player 11 recognizes the device without any intervention from you.

So, without further ado, open Media Player 11, plug your device into the USB port of your PC, and watch while Windows Vista and Media Player 11 install and recognize it. (If for some reason this doesn't happen automatically, you'll be prompted to either install the disc that came with the device or let Windows Vista go online to try to find an appropriate driver for it.)

## UNDERSTAND PLAYSFORSURE

When shopping for your first portable music device, or if you're in the market for a new one, look for the PlaysForSure logo. With a PlaysForSure-branded device, you can be sure that the one you get will be compatible with Media Player 11, Windows Vista, and URGE. PlaysForSure devices are also compatible with other online stores including CinemaNow, MSN Music, Musicmatch, Music Now, Napster, and many more. You can find the PlaysForSure logo on lots of device too, including portable video players, digital audio receivers, Pocket PCs, and smartphones.

## SYNC A MOBILE DEVICE

 **10 minutes**

To *sync* Media Player 11 means to copy media files from your player's library to a portable music device (or vice versa). Your portable music device may be a small keychain-type device like a simple USB flash drive, a larger portable music player like Zune, a larger digital media player, or even a Pocket PC or smartphone. As long as the device is compatible with Media Player 11 and Windows Vista, it doesn't matter what it is!

Devices come in all sizes (as well as all shapes). If your device can hold at least 4GB of data and if your entire Media Player 11 library can fit on the device, Media Player 11 will automatically copy your media the first time you connect it to sync. (If it can't hold your entire library or isn't 4GB, you'll be prompted to sync manually, by hand-picking the media you want on it.) Each time you sync after the initial sync, Media Player 11 updates the device to mirror your library.

To perform a sync for the first time, follow these steps:

1. Start Media Player 11, and connect the device.

2. If an automatic sync occurs, simply wait until it's finished, and click Finish.

3. If you're prompted to create a manual sync, select the Sync tab.

4. Browse through your media library, and drop songs you want on the device to the Sync pane.

5. Once you've added all the songs, click Start Sync.

You can watch the sync in progress! To sync from here on, simply connect the device.

# STREAM MUSIC THROUGH YOUR HOME

It's possible to stream music from your PC to other rooms in the home by using your wired or wireless home network. This means you don't have to put your PC in the main room just to listen to music there, and you don't have to run speaker wire through the attic! With Windows Vista, Media Player 11, and a networked digital media player (more about that later), you can leave your computer in your home office and play music in any room your home.

## KNOW WHAT YOU'LL NEED

If you want to stream music throughout your home, you're going to need two things:

**A network**   You'll need an Ethernet or wireless home network, so if you don't have one, you'll need to set one up.

**A digital media extender**   You'll need a digital media extender, such as an Xbox 360, Roku SoundBridge, or D-Link MediaLounge DSM-320. These three options work great with Media Player 11. This is what lets you play music that's on your computer in another room in the house. (If you get a different brand of player, the setup is pretty much the same, though.)

## CONNECT AN XBOX (OR OTHER DIGITAL MEDIA PLAYER) TO A HOME NETWORK

 **30 minutes to 1 hour**

The first step in streaming music throughout your home is to set up your digital media player. No matter which device you choose, the setup is basically the same.

If you have a wired network, connect your digital media player to your home network by using an Ethernet cable that's long enough to reach the network router. This sort of setup undermines the magic of streaming music throughout your home, though, because you still end up stringing a long cable in the attic or around the baseboards. However, it is one way.

If you have a wireless network, you can stream music without the hassle of wires. To connect your Xbox 360 or similar device to a wireless network, follow these steps:

1. Turn on the router or access point.

2. Plug the Xbox 360's wireless adapter into the USB port on the Xbox console.

3. From the console's dashboard, click System.

4. Click Network Settings, click Edit Settings, and click Wireless Mode.

5. Select your wireless network from the list, and click Done.

## TURN ON MEDIA SHARING

To share your music with your wired or wireless network devices, you have to turn on media sharing in Media Player 11. To turn on media sharing, follow these steps:

1. Open Media Player 11, and click the arrow on the Library tab.

2. Click Media Sharing, as shown in Figure 7-3.

3. In the Sharing Settings dialog box, click Share My Media. You can leave Find Media That Others Are Sharing selected. Click OK.

4. In the Media Sharing dialog box, select the digital media device you installed. Click OK.

**Figure 7-3:** To share the media on your PC with your digital media device, you have to click Media Sharing on the Library tab menu.

## PLAY SHARED MEDIA

Once you've installed your digital media player and turned on media sharing, you're ready to enjoy music on your new device. The process differs depending on what device you installed; however, for the most part, you'll follow these steps:

1. Use the digital media recorder's remote control to select the name of the computer on the network that holds the music you want to hear.

2. Browse through the media you want to play, and select any song, playlist, or album.

3. Enjoy!

# Get the Most from Your High-End Speakers

If the speakers connected to your PC are high-definition speakers, you can configure those speakers for better performance by working through the advanced sound
options available in Windows Vista. Figure 7-4 shows these options, which are available on the Enhancements tab of the Speakers dialog box; Loudness Equalization is
selected here.

These new options include the following:

**Bass Management** Select Bass Management if you have a separate, large
subwoofer, one that's capable of handling
loud, low, bass sounds better than your
smaller speakers.

**Speaker Fill** Select Speaker Fill if you
have more speakers than available music
channels. For instance, if you have media
recorded in stereo (two speakers) but you
have five speakers, Speaker Fill will adjust
the playback to incorporate the additional
speakers effectively.

**Room Correction** Select this to find
your room's "sweet spot" for sound. You'll
need a microphone to tell Windows Vista
where you'd like to sit and then run a cali-
bration wizard to guide you through the
process of finding just the right sound.

**Figure 7-4:** If you have high-definition speakers, you'll see a
few new features on the Enhancements tab in the Speakers
dialog box, including Bass Management, Speaker Fill, Room
Correction, and Loudness Equalization.

**Loudness Equalization** Select Loudness Equalization if the media you're
listening to has big differences between the loud and soft parts of the
movie, song, or other media. This is a great feature for watching television,
because the commercials are quite a bit louder than the programming.

If you don't have the required hardware, you won't have access to these additional options. To see whether your speakers are considered a "high-definition" audio device (and to find out whether you have access to these additional options), follow these steps:

1. Right-click the Sound icon in the Notification area of the taskbar, and click Playback Devices. If you don't see the Sound icon (it looks like a speaker), click Start, Control Panel, Hardware And Sound, Sound.

2. On the Playback tab, double-click the speakers you use to play the music you listen to in Media Player 11. (You may see more than one option for playback.)

3. If you have desktop speakers, you'll see three tabs, as shown in Figure 7-5: General, Levels, and Advanced. If you have high-end speakers, you'll see an additional tab, Enhancements, as shown in Figure 7-4 earlier.

Figure 7-5: You'll see only three tabs and won't have access to the new sound enhancements if you're using regular desktop speakers.

In this chapter, you learned how to work with music when you're away from your PC. Specifically, you learned how to get music online and then take it with you on a portable device. You also learned the basics for listening to music throughout your home by streaming it through your network. Finally, you learned how to get the most from your high-end speakers.

# PART IV Video

- Get an overview of Windows Movie Maker

- Create your video library

- Learn about video formats

- Import existing videos

- Send and receive e-mail with video attachments

# **Fine-Tune** Your Video Library

# CHAPTER 8

If you're like us, you're guilty of taking lots of pictures and home videos and then shoving them all into a drawer to be viewed "someday." Chances are, someday never arrives because the thought of digging through all that stuff is just too overwhelming. Now, however, you have a nifty little helper in the Windows Vista operating system. Depending on the amount of stuff crammed into your drawer, you can be watching movies of your memories after less than an afternoon in front of your computer. At the same time, you'll have fun—Windows Vista takes what used to be manual drudgery and turns it into creative, high-tech entertainment through the extensive use of click-and-drag options and ready-to-use effects and transitions.

# Get an Overview of Windows Movie Maker

*You can capture content in a variety of ways—direct from a digital video camera, imported from existing video files or still pictures, or even converted from analog video files.*

Windows Movie Maker is a cool Windows Vista tool. With it, you are the director, editor, cinematographer, and distributor of your own movies. You can capture content in a variety of ways—direct from a digital video camera, imported from existing video files or still pictures, or even converted from analog video files. Then, add titles, transitions, and effects, and *voila*! Your very own movie is ready to share with friends and family. Probably the only real problem you'll have is making sure they have a decent media player installed on their computers so they can see your handiwork. (Hey! Give them Windows Vista on their next birthday!)

Windows Movie Maker has a user interface that's easy to use. Different panes appear depending upon the view you are in—the Collections view or the Tasks view. You can change your view by clicking the View menu and clicking the view you want. The Collections view will display your clips in collections; they are displayed by name in the left pane and by clip in the right pane. Incidentally, this view is actually a database file with a .dat extension that stores information about how your collection is organized, as well as the clips within the collection. A collection file is created for every user account.

The Tasks view will display common tasks performed when making movies, such as Import, Edit, and Publish To (see Figure 8-1). Clicking some tasks will open a dialog box, while others will simply guide you through a specific task. Other panes are the Contents pane, which shows files, clips, effects and transitions, and the Preview Monitor pane, which lets you view individual clips or an entire project.

At the bottom of your screen, you'll notice the Storyboard/Timeline pane. This pane is where you will manage your movie: Storyboard (the default pane) lets you see and rearrange the sequence, effects, and transition of your clips. The name comes from the storyboard

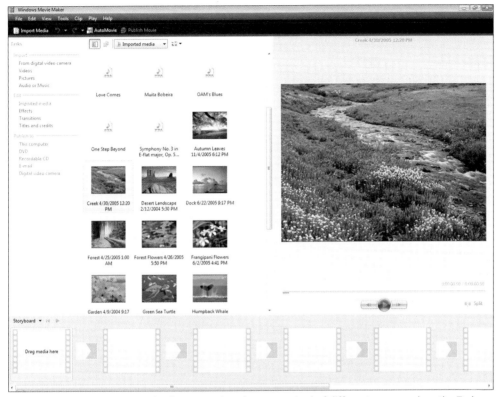

**Figure 8-1:** Windows Movie Maker has a user interface comprised of different panes such as the Tasks view on the left. At a glance, you can see different aspects of your video and make changes as required.

concept used in the film industry—back in the day, filmmakers drew these story-boards by hand to help determine the proper sequence of scenes and effects. It's not nearly that complicated for you. You'll just click and drag clips to the Storyboard pane, and if you don't like where you placed them, you can drag them to new loca-tions until you're happy—no erasers needed.

If you switch to the Timeline pane, you can review and modify the timing of clips just like a movie director—zoom in or out, record narrations, adjust audio levels, and so on. It's almost silly how easy it is to make these additions and changes, as you'll discover. But that's the beauty of Windows Vista.

# Create Your Video Library

Your video library is just a database that contains links to video files on your computer; it does not actually contain your files. It is located in your Windows Media Player and links to videos, music, and picture files. You can place your own videos in the library, or you can download video files from online stores within the player. The library doesn't care where they come from; it just wants to know what you want in there.

This is probably the part of the afternoon that will take you the longest. You need to decide which files you want in your library, and then you need to locate them and possibly download them. All these tasks can take time, so maybe you should grab a cup of coffee or a diet soda and settle in. To help you organize your thoughts and pare down the media as you sort through your media files, ask yourself these questions:

- Will someone be able to blackmail me with this when I become famous?
- Will anyone other than Grandma want to see this?
- How often will I really pull this out to embarrass my child?
- Do I need to document this moment for legal reasons?

Once you've answered key questions about the media file involved and have decided to keep it, you're ready to rumble.

# Find Videos in Your Media Player Library

Finding videos can be a time-consuming process if you have them stashed all over your computer. For most people, though, this will be a pretty simple procedure.

 5 minutes

1. Click the arrow on the Library tab in Media Player.
2. Click Video.
3. In the left Navigation pane, locate and select your video by category (Recently Added, All Video, Actors, Genre, Rating). Figure 8-2 shows the videos organized by length.

**Figure 8-2:** The Media Player Library tab offers you several different ways to locate and organize your videos.

If you select the All Video category, notice that above the video files is a taskbar with gray text. Click a gray word (Title, Length, Release Year, and so on), and watch how the information next to the file changes. Next, let's make sure your video library is ready to go with video files you can create or edit using Windows Movie Maker.

# Understand Video Formats

You should consider a few issues before you get started for the afternoon. Video format decisions are important in your video library because the *type* of format you choose determines the video file type for the resulting video when you use the

Import Video command. You can import video from a videotape in one of two ways: as a Windows Media Video (WMV) file or as the default format from your digital video (DV) device.

Table 8-1 offers some items to consider when choosing a video format.

| CONSIDERATION | VIDEO FORMAT TO USE |
|---|---|
| Which video-editing program will you use to edit the imported video? | Use a video format supported by the editing program you have. |
| Are you planning to record your final movie to videotape? | Use Video Device Format (AVI). |
| How much disk space do you have? | Match the format to your available space. AVI files, for example, consume about 13GB of disk space for every hour of video, while WMV files consume just 1GB for the same hour. |
| What is the aspect ratio of the original video? | Choose a video format and aspect ratio that is the same as the recorded video on the tape. |
| Will you allow dropped frames? | If you will, choose AVI format. If you will not, choose WMV format. |

**Table 8-1:**
Choosing a
video format

You have two basic aspect ratios to consider with your movies. An *aspect ratio* is the relation of width to height on the video display—how your video will actually display in your final published movie. If you want your movie to display like the full-screen view of a standard television, use the 4:3 aspect ratio. If you prefer a widescreen appearance (which typically displays black bars at the top and bottom), then choose the 16:9 aspect ratio. You can have both in your video library, of course, but if you plan to mix and reuse clips much, it's a good idea to stick to one aspect ratio in order to keep files at reasonable numbers.

## CREATE MULTIPLE VIDEO FILES DURING IMPORT

Sometimes, Windows Movie Maker will create more than one video file when you import a video from videotape. This isn't necessarily a problem, but it's important to know about it so you can be sure to track all your files. Windows Movie Maker will create multiple files when the format of the video on the tape changes or when the aspect ratio of the video on the tape changes. For each of these scenarios, Windows Movie Maker will create a new file every time a change takes place.

## Import Existing Videos

You may have videos in a variety of formats, and that's okay. Windows Movie Maker accepts most of them.

 **10 minutes per video (on average)**

You can import the following digital video file types into Windows Movie Maker by default:

| | |
|---|---|
| .asf | .mpe |
| .avi | .mpg |
| .m1v | .mpv2 |
| .mp2 | .wm |
| .mp2v | .wmv |
| .mpeg | |

You can import videos from your digital camera (explained in more detail in Chapter 9) as well as use Windows Easy Transfer to import existing video files to your new computer, as explained in Chapter 2. If you have video files to import from your network or don't want to use Windows Easy Transfer, don't sweat it. It's really easy to do in Windows Movie Maker. Are you ready?

## IMPORT A VIDEO FROM A FILE

If your video is located on your computer, you follow a slightly different process than you would if it were on a CD or DVD.

 **2 minutes per video**

1. In Windows Movie Maker, click File.

2. Click Import Media Items.

3. In the Import Media Items dialog box that appears, locate and select the video you want to import.

   - In the left Favorite Links pane, notice the Video link. This is the default location where Windows Vista will take you so you can locate your video. If your video is located elsewhere, click a different link.

   - Type the path and filename in the File Name box if you know them to find your file quickly.

   - Click All Media Files, and use the drop-down list to narrow the search if you want.

4. Click Import.

Your video will appear in Windows Movie Maker.

## IMPORT A VIDEO FROM A CD OR DVD

Now you'll learn how to import a video from a CD or DVD. Notice that starting with step 3, this import process differs from importing video from a file. It doesn't really take much longer, however.

 **3 minutes per video**

1. In Windows Movie Maker, click File.

2. Click Import Media Items, as shown in Figure 8-3.

3. In the Import Media Items dialog box that appears, click Computer in the Favorite Links pane.

④ In Devices With Removable Storage, double-click your DVD drive.

⑤ Locate and select the video you want to import.

- Type the path and filename in the File Name box if you know them to find your file quickly.

- Click All Media Files, and use the drop-down list to narrow the search if you want.

⑥ Click Import.

Your video will appear in Windows Movie Maker.

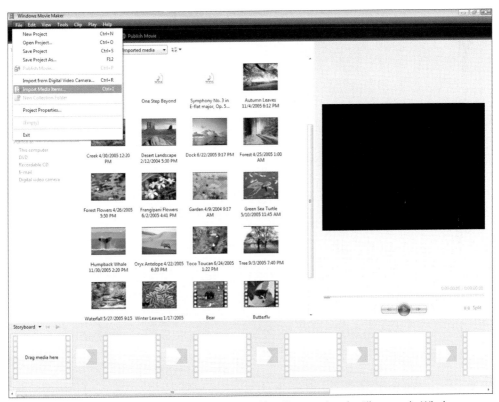

**Figure 8-3:** You can import existing videos into your video library using the File menu in Windows Movie Maker.

## UNDERSTAND TYPICAL ERROR MESSAGES

When you import video, you may sometimes see an error message. The most common errors involve digital rights management (DRM) and unsupported video file formats. DRM errors are triggered when copyright protections are in place—you cannot import protected DRM files into Windows Movie Maker. Unsupported video format errors occur when you try to import a file format that is not recognized by Windows Movie Maker. If this type of error occurs, try converting the file into a format that Windows Movie Maker supports. You can do this using a non-Microsoft video-editing program; then try importing the file again.

# Send and Receive E-Mail with Video Attachments

If you have a video that you are ready to send—or you are receiving videos from others as e-mail attachments—then take a minute to read this section.

When you receive a video attachment in an e-mail, it's critical to verify that the sender and the attachment are known and expected. Dangerous file types are often blocked by Windows Mail, but occasionally, something can slip through. Opening an attachment without confirming its origins can open your system up to worms, Trojans, and other attacks. These are malicious programs that use your computer for a variety of bad actions. Of course, there are more technical explanations for them, but the bottom line is that the more you can avoid them, the better.

Next, ask yourself whether you really need to keep this attachment. Do you need this video to help with building other videos? Or is this just a file to read and toss? If you don't need the file, delete the entire message to keep plenty of room available in your e-mail archives.

Sometimes when you try to open an attachment, you can't. This may be because Windows Mail has blocked it. New security aspects in Windows Vista block certain types of file attachments, such as .exe., .pif, and .scr files, that are known to spread viruses. If Windows Mail has blocked an attachment, the Information bar will display a message advising you.

## OPEN AND SAVE A VIDEO OR OTHER MEDIA E-MAIL ATTACHMENT

Remember, never open an attachment if you aren't certain about its origin. We can't stress this enough!

 **1 minute (or more if the attachment is large)**

1. Open Windows Mail.

2. Open the message containing the attachment.

3. In the message window, click the File menu.

4. Click Save Attachments.

5. Select the folders where you want to save the attachments.

   Windows Mail by default will save the attachment in your Documents folder.

6. Select the attachment you want to save.

7. Click Save.

# SEND VIDEO ATTACHMENTS

When sending a video as an e-mail attachment, keep in mind that most e-mail providers impose file size limits on incoming mail. This limit is typically from 1MB to 2MB per message. If your file is larger than that, consider sending it via "snail mail" rather than e-mail. Although individual pictures can be automatically resized in Windows Photo Gallery for e-mail, videos cannot.

# CONVERT YOUR OLD ANALOG TAPES TO DIGITAL FORMAT

If you have home videos on analog tape, you might want to consider converting them to digital format pretty soon. Although digital formats may change in the coming years (of course they will!), it's clear analog is not making a comeback any-time soon. And for those of us old enough to remember the Beta/VHS wars, well, let's just say anyone still holding onto a Beta tape is either extremely stubborn or trapped in a time warp. (If you still have LPs, though, it's actually a badge of honor. Albums are cool!)

Seriously, don't let yourself become the butt of analog jokes; make your getaway while it still seems reasonable to have a relic in your video archives. Although the conversions may not be perfect quality, they will still be better than having no video at all—and that's the alternative not too far down the road. You can convert these old tapes in a couple of ways; the following are the highlights. If you don't have the equipment mentioned, head to your local high-tech store, and get one before you lose precious memories.

## USE AN ANALOG-TO-DV CONVERTER

Using an analog-to-DV converter offers the most flexibility when converting your tapes. This kind of converter captures VHS video directly to your computer's video-editing program, which means you can edit the video as you make the conversion. However, it is also the most time-consuming method because you have to encode the video to MPEG-2 and then author a DVD.

## USE A HARDWARE ANALOG-TO-MPEG CAPTURE DEVICE

With this method, you can capture your video directly to your computer. You have limited flexibility, but this is a quick way to make the conversion, and it offers pretty decent quality. You can usually at least add a DVD menu to the video.

## USE A CAMCORDER AND STAND-ALONE DVD RECORDER

This option is really just a DVD copy of your tape; there is little flexibility, and it's unlikely you can add a DVD menu using this method. However, it is hands-down the fastest method of conversion available today.

This chapter gave you an overview of how to begin using Windows Movie Maker and work with your video library. Choosing the right video format is a critical decision, with a variety of issues to consider. You can build your Media Player video library by importing existing videos, which may already be on your computer or may come to you through e-mail.

- Connect your camera
- Import your video
- Make a movie with Movie Maker

# **Import** Video and Make a Quick Movie

# CHAPTER 9

Anyone who has taken a movie on their digital camera or video camera and then put the tape away into a drawer and never looked at it again should read this chapter. There's nothing worse than capturing memories and then losing them to the junk drawer. It's so ridiculously easy to import video and make a movie to send to all your friends and family—or view whenever you want—with the Windows Vista operating system that you'll wonder why it seemed so difficult before. You'll have a few hardware issues to tackle, but once you've resolved them, you should be making movies easily. Get your camera, put on your creative hat, and let's roll tape. (That's a movie phrase every director should know.)

# Connect the Camera

 **10 minutes**

In the previous chapter, you learned the basics of Windows Movie Maker. You've taken some raw footage with your digital camera, and now it's time make a movie! The first step is to connect your camera to your computer so you can import the video.

You can connect digital video (DV) cameras to your computer in two ways: through an IEEE 1394 connection or through a USB 2.0 connection. The IEEE 1394 connection method is the most popular, but both import video equally well and use the same process.

You must have the proper *drivers*—software that lets your camera communicate with your computer—installed on your computer before your camera can connect properly. This software typically comes with the camera on the installation CD, so be sure you have installed this before attempting to connect your camera to your computer. You can also set Windows Vista to automatically notify you when new drivers are available for your hardware. Drivers are not updated automatically, but Windows Update can notify you when new drivers become available for you to then update.

*It's so ridiculously easy to import video and make a movie to send to all your friends and family—or view whenever you want—with Windows Vista that you'll wonder why it seemed so difficult before.*

### VERIFY WINDOWS UPDATE IS SET TO NOTIFY YOU OF DRIVER UPDATES

To verify that Windows Update will notify you when driver updates are available, follow these steps:

1. Click the Start button, and click Control Panel.
2. Open Windows Update.
3. Click Change Settings.
4. Be sure Install Updates Automatically is selected.
5. In the Recommended Updates section, verify the Include Recommended Updates When Downloading, Installing, Or Notifying Me About Updates check box is selected.
6. Click OK.

**TROUBLESHOOTING** You may be asked for an administrator password or be restricted from making changes because of your network security settings. If this happens, contact your administrator.

## CONNECT A CAMERA BY USING AN IEEE 1394 OR USB CONNECTION

Always refer to your manufacturer's instructions, and follow them if they differ from the instructions here. Most camera connections will follow these steps:

1. Plug the cable into the DV or USB 2.0 port on your camera.

2. Plug the other end of the cable into the IEEE 1394 or USB 2.0 port on your computer.

   The first time you plug in the camera, Windows Vista will install the driver software for it—even if you have already installed it. Don't be alarmed if it takes a minute or two for the connection to occur.

3. Turn on the camera, and set your camera mode to record live video (sometimes labeled Camera, but your setting may be different).

4. Go to the import instructions in the "Perform the Import" section.

# CAMERA CONNECTION TROUBLESHOOTING

If you have connected your camera to your computer but nothing happens or you can't find your pictures, ask yourself these questions:

- Is your camera turned on? (Turn on the camera.)
- Does your camera have a special connection mode that needs to be turned on? (Switch to the correct connection setting.)
- Do you have the correct drivers for your camera? (Go to your camera's manufacturer Web site or the installation disc, and install the drivers again.)
- Is the computer port working? (Try a different port to see whether the camera works from the new port.)
- Is the flash memory card in the camera? (Insert it if it is not there.)

# Perform the Import

**15 minutes**

Once you are ready to import video, you can do it in three ways: directly from the camera to your computer, through Windows Movie Maker (as shown in Figure 9-1), or through Windows Photo Gallery. We'll focus on the direct-to-computer and Windows Movie Maker methods here.

When you import videos, the video is saved to your computer's hard drive as a video file. You can edit the saved file by using Windows Movie Maker.

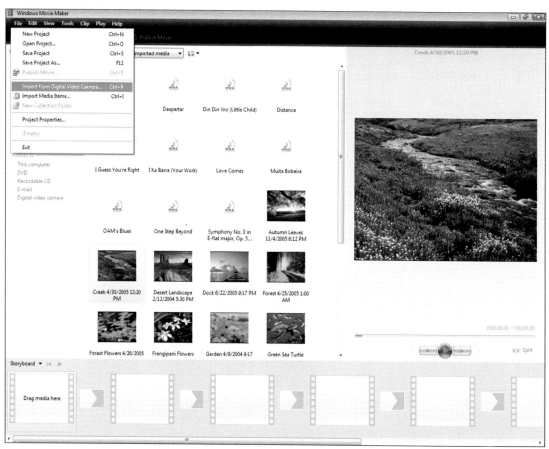

**Figure 9-1:** You can import live and taped video from a variety of places, including your digital video camera.

## IMPORT LIVE VIDEO FROM A DV CAMERA

Be sure to remove any videotape from the camera before beginning this process. If you don't, your camera may go into standby mode—this will stop the import process, and you'll have to start all over again. Then follow these steps:

1. Once you properly connect your camera to your computer, the Import Video Wizard opens automatically. Click Import Video.

2. Type a name for the video file.

3. From Import To List or Browse, choose a location to which to save your file.

4. Select a video file format. Click Next.

5. Click Start Video Import.

6. Wait the specified amount of time for the live video to be imported, or click Stop Video Import.

7. Click Finish.

## IMPORT ALL OF A TAPED VIDEO FROM A DV CAMERA

To import all of a taped video from your DV camera, follow these steps:

1. Once you properly connect your camera to your computer, the Import Video Wizard opens automatically. Click Import Video.

2. Type a name for the video file.

3. From Import To List or Browse, choose a location to which to save your file.

4. Select a video file format. Click Next.

5. Click Import The Entire Videotape To My Computer.

6. Click Next.

## IMPORT A PORTION OF A TAPED VIDEO FROM A DV CAMERA

To import a portion of a taped video from your DV camera, follow these steps:

1. Once you properly connect your camera to your computer, the Import Video Wizard opens automatically. Click Import Video.

2. Type a name for the video file.

3. From Import to List or Browse, choose a location to which to save your file.

4. Choose a video file format. Click Next.

5. Click Only Import Parts Of The Videotape To My Computer.

6. Click Next.

7. In the Cue The Videotape And Then Start Importing Video dialog box, do one or both of the following:

   - Locate the start of the clip or clips you want to import by using the DV camera controls in Import Video or the controls on your DV camera.

   - Specify an amount of time for the video to import by selecting the Stop Importing After check box and typing a time limit.

8. Click Start Video Import.

9. Click Stop Video Import, or wait for the specified time limit for the video to download.

10. Click Finish.

Windows Movie Maker does not support importing video from a Web camera. Use a DV camera or a digital camera that records video instead.

# IS THE IMPORT REALLY FINISHED?

Before you unplug your camera, be absolutely certain it has finished downloading your video. If your camera has an activity light, wait until it stops blinking before unplugging the camera. Another way to tell is that a Safely Remove Hardware icon will appear in the Notification area at the far right of your taskbar. You can click this icon for a list of devices and then click the device you want to remove.

# Make a Movie with Movie Maker

 **45 minutes**

Now that you have imported video to your computer and saved it to a location that works well for you, you're ready to turn that raw footage into a movie! You can do this in two ways in Windows Movie Maker: You can use AutoMovie or create your movie manually.

AutoMovie is the best choice if you are a novice at making movies. It will analyze your videos, pictures, and music and then combine everything to make a movie based on the editing style you select. If you have made movies before, you might prefer to create your movie manually. This gives you more control in handling details and creating a final product that meets your exact specifications.

No matter which movie-making method you choose, you are not limited to the transitions and effects that come with Movie Maker. Windows Media Player 11 offers an online store that sells digital media content by subscription. You can find and subscribe to music, video, radio services, and other content; the content is typically protected by copyright and media usage rights that may specify how you can use the content.

## BROWSE IN ONLINE STORES FOR CONTENT

To browse in online stores for content, follow these steps:

1. Open Media Player 11. Click the down arrow below the URGE icon on the toolbar.

2. In the menu that opens, click Browse All Online Stores.

A Web page will display the list of stores available. Click the store in which you are interested. A prompt will ask you to verify you want to shop at the store. Click Yes, and begin shopping.

## CREATE A MOVIE WITH AUTOMOVIE

When you create a movie with AutoMovie, keep these points in mind:

- The collection or group of files used must contain video, audio, pictures, or a combination of all these that is at least 30 seconds in duration.

- Movie Maker will assign each picture a duration of four seconds.

To create the movie with AutoMovie, follow these steps:

1. Open Movie Maker, and click the collection where your movie or multiple clips are stored.

2. Click Tools, AutoMovie.

3. Select an editing style from the list provided, as shown in Figure 9-2.

4. Under More Options, click Enter A Title For The Movie. Type the title in the text box.

5. Under More Options, click Select Audio Or Background Music.

   - Click the box under Audio And Music Files to expand the list, or click Browse to find a different audio or music file. Click None if you do not want audio or music.

   - Verify the audio level, and move the slider from Video to Audio or from Video to Audio/Music to increase the volume one way or the other.

6. Click Create AutoMovie. The movie will appear on your screen.

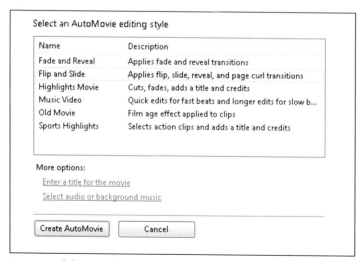

Figure 9-2: Select an editing style to have AutoMovie analyze your video, audio, and pictures and turn them into a movie for you.

## CREATE A MOVIE MANUALLY

If you've made movies before and are confident enough to create a movie manually, we'll assume you already know what transitions, titles, and effects are. The process of making a movie manually is to use the Storyboard pane (Figure 9-3) to place your clips where you want them and the Timeline pane (Figure 9-4) to determine the duration of the clips within the Storyboard pane. You can start with either the Storyboard pane or the Timeline pane; our instructions will use the Storyboard pane as the foundation for the project.

**Figure 9-3:** The Storyboard pane lets you see all your clips, transitions, and effects at once. You can click and drag to make changes directly on the Storyboard pane.

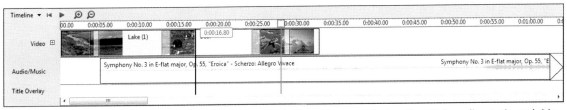

**Figure 9-4:** The Timeline pane lets you see how the timing of all your items works together. Only audio, music, and title information is available in this pane.

To make a movie manually, follow these steps:

1. Click View, Storyboard And Collections.

2. Click File, New Project.

3. In the Collections pane, select the imported media, transitions, and effects you want to use:

   - From the Imported Media collection you choose, drag the media clips you want to use to the Storyboard pane. Notice that imported media is dropped automatically into the large placeholders on the Storyboard pane.

- From the Transitions collection, drag the transition you want to the medium placeholder box between the media clips.

- From the Effects collection, drag the effect you want to the small box located in the lower-right corner of your media clip placeholder.

④ Click Play, Play Storyboard, or click the Play button.

If you are happy with the storyboard, continue to step 5. If not, delete the clips, transitions, and effects, and repeat all parts of step 3 until you are satisfied.

⑤ Click Tools, Titles And Credits. Add titles and credits with the options provided.

⑥ Click File, Save Project.

⑦ Type a file name, and click Save, making sure the file type is Windows Movie Maker Projects.

# DRAG ITEMS TO THE STORYBOARD PANE

Movie Maker doesn't let you keep blank placeholders. As you drag items to the Storyboard pane, you will notice that even if you choose a specific placeholder for the item, if there is a blank one before it, Movie Maker will drop the item on the first available blank placeholder.

## ADD AUDIO CLIPS TO YOUR MOVIE

You can add audio clips only in the Timeline pane. Click View, Timeline, and then drag the audio clip to the Timeline pane where you want it.

## SAVE OFTEN!

You'll notice that we don't tell you to save your work in the instructions. That's because you will actually be publishing the movie to your computer (or elsewhere) when it's complete rather than saving it to your computer. But you should save often when working on your movie by clicking File, Save (or Save As) to ensure your hard work doesn't go down the drain before your movie is published.

Add a tag to your file to make it easier to find—select the Tags box in the Save As dialog box, and type one or more tags separated by semicolons. You can add other files properties here too, such as Rating, Title, and Author.

### PUBLISH A MOVIE TO YOUR COMPUTER

When you have completed your movie, it's time to publish it. When it's published, you can share it with other people through your computer, on a CD, as an attachment in an e-mail, or on videotape in a DV camera. We'll explain the steps for publishing to your computer here; use Movie Maker Help if you prefer to publish it to another medium:

1. Click File, Publish Movie.
2. Select This Computer, and click Next.
3. Type a name for your movie in the File Name box.
4. Choose a Publish To path by using the drop-down menu or the Browse button. Click Next.

⑤ In Choose The Settings For Your Movie, select a setting, and click Publish.

At the bottom of this window, notice how the Movie Settings And File Size Information details change as you make different setting selections.

⑥ Click Publish.

⑦ Select Play Movie When I Click Finish if you want to see the movie immediately.

⑧ Click Finish.

## REMOVE EXTRA FOOTAGE

If you have extra footage you don't need, it's easy to remove it through a process called *splitting*. When you split a video, you divide it into two parts. As the video plays, you simply click the Split button at the bottom right of the video (to the far right of the Play button), as shown in Figure 9-5. Wherever you click the Split button is where the video will be cut in two.

**Figure 9-5:** You can easily get rid of extra video by clicking the Split button, located to the far right of the Play button.

The two videos will now appear in your collection. If you have more pieces of the video to remove, use the splitting process until you have the clips you want. When you're done splitting, follow these steps:

① Right-click the clip in your collection.

② Click Cut.

> **TIP** Keep track of the number of splits by renaming your new clips as you go. Movie Maker will number them, but if you have several splits, it's easy to get lost and forget which split contained the video you want to keep.

Creativity will breed dozens of ways to capture memories in movies that are bound to entertain family and friends for years. Now that you know the basics of connecting your camera and importing video, take some time to familiarize yourself with all the wonderful features, effects, and transitions Movie Maker offers. The most important requirement is to have fun! You'll be glad you took the time when you view these movies years from now.

- Burn your own home-movie DVD

- Publish your movie to the Web

# **Do** Two Simple Video Projects in One Hour

# CHAPTER 10

Although plenty of geeks like us are left on the planet, we admit "regular" people don't have a lot of time to spend in front of the computer. That doesn't mean you can't have the cool stuff we geeks have, though! In some ways, the Windows Vista operating system takes the fun out of geekdom—there's little left that we can use to act superior to novices. Burning DVDs and publishing movies to Web sites are some of the cool tasks you can do in an hour or less by using Windows Vista. Yes. Less than an hour. Even if you are technically challenged, you too can accomplish these tasks in less than an hour.

Pardon us while we cry. Is there nothing sacred left for the geeks? Weren't we supposed to inherit the earth? Oh, wait—that's the meek, not the geek....

# Burn Your Own Home-Movie DVD

**Burning DVDs and publishing movies to Web sites are some of the cool tasks you can do in an hour or less by using Windows Vista.**

**30 minutes or less**

Okay, so burning a DVD sounds a little frightening if you haven't done it before. But rest assured, this process doesn't involve flames or smoke (unless you have a cigarette in hand). To get started, you need have Windows DVD Maker open:

**1** Click Start.

**2** Click All Programs.

**3** Click Windows DVD Maker. This opens the Add Pictures And Video To The DVD dialog box, as shown in Figure 10-1.

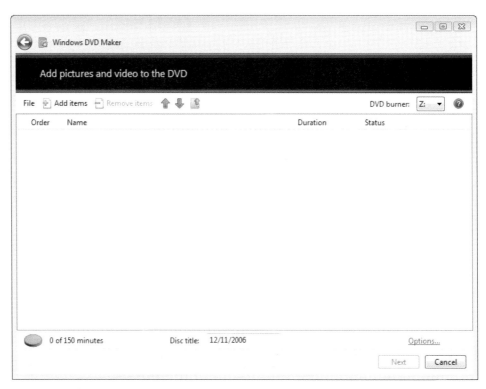

**Figure 10-1:** When you open DVD Maker, the Add Pictures And Video To The DVD dialog box appears.

Figure 10-2: The AutoPlay dialog box appears when you insert a DVD into the drive.

**TIP** If you prefer, you can simply insert a blank recordable or rewritable DVD into your DVD drive. Give it a minute, and then the AutoPlay dialog box will appear, as shown in Figure 10-2. Just click Burn A DVD Video Disc Using Windows DVD Maker.

## ADD PICTURES OR VIDEO TO A DVD

Next, you have to figure out what you want to place on the DVD. Ask yourself, why am I spending time inside when I could be swimming, hiking, or doing any number of activities that don't involve sitting? Am I just lazy, or do I have a point here? Assuming you have a point to making this DVD, follow these steps:

1 Click Add Items in the Add Pictures And Video To The DVD dialog box.

2 In the Add Items To DVD dialog box, locate the items you want to place on the DVD. Don't worry about order at this point. Taking a lot of time here just makes the task longer. We're not trying to scare you; we're just reminding you that indecision will make this process longer than 30 minutes.

**TIP** You can add multiple items by clicking the first item, holding down Ctrl, and clicking additional items.

**③** Click Add. The selected items will appear in the Add Pictures And Video To The DVD dialog box.

**④** Now, think about the order you want these items to play. If you need to move any up or down, click the item, and use the Up and Down arrows in the toolbar.

- You can also drag items up and down.

- If you need to remove an item, select it, and click Remove Items.

**⑤** Click Next.

This next step is so simple that it's easy to overlook. But when you play a DVD purchased from a store, there is a menu for you to use, right? You need to determine here whether you want to add a menu to your DVD and where you want it—at the beginning or the end of your DVD. If you don't want to add one, you can simply choose to have your video loop continuously. You also need to choose the aspect ratio (discussed in Chapter 8) and the format. So, you need to select some options before actually burning the DVD.

## ADDING DVD OPTIONS

To set some options for the DVD, follow these steps:

**①** Click Options in the Add Pictures And Video To The DVD dialog box.

**②** Choose your DVD playback settings, aspect ratio, and video format by selecting the appropriate option, as shown in Figure 10-3.

**③** Choose a temporary file location by clicking the Browse button. Unless you really want your DVD to burn slowly, don't bother changing the burner speed.

**④** Click OK.

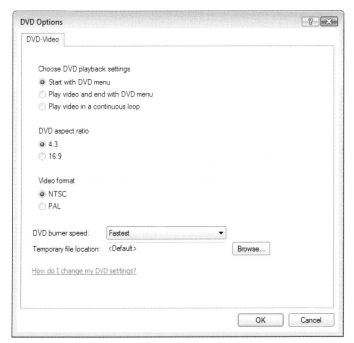

**Figure 10-3:** You can set some DVD options after you select the items to burn to your DVD.

> **NOTE** You can still see a menu if you choose to play your video continuously in a loop—use the remote control.

Now you should be back at the Add Pictures And Video To The DVD dialog box. Don't worry—you're leaving it soon. But since you're here, verify your DVD burner is correct (some people have more than one DVD burner). Once you're satisfied it's correct, scan down to the bottom of the dialog box, and find Disc Title. Type a new title here, unless you like the one the program assigned.

Now you can leave this dialog box by clicking Next.

## SET MENU TEXT AND STYLES

Settle down—you're not ready to burn the disc just yet, even though the dialog box seems to indicate that. You have a couple of housekeeping items to take care of in the Ready To Burn Disc dialog box:

❶ Click Menu Text. Make changes as desired. Click Change Text if you made changes; click Don't Change if you didn't.

❷ Click Customize Menu. Make changes as desired. Click Change Style if you made changes; click Don't Change if you didn't.

To see how your menu text will look when you actually burn the DVD, click Preview. Click OK when you're ready to exit the preview.

## SPECIFY SLIDE-SHOW SETTINGS

If you are burning photos to your DVD, you need to set photo settings for the slide show. In the Ready To Burn Disc dialog box, follow these steps:

❶ Click Slide Show.

❷ In the Change Your Slide Show Settings dialog box, you have a lot of options:

- You can add music with the Add Music button.

- You can change the slide show length to match the length of your music selection.

- You can select the time your pictures will display (unless you selected a slide show length to match the music length).

- You can choose transition settings.

- You can add pan and zoom effects.

❸ When you have made your selections, click Change Slide Show. If you didn't make any selections, click Don't Change.

## BURN YOUR DVD

*Now* it's time to actually burn your items to DVD. By now, you should have spent just about 20 minutes fiddling around with text, style, and slide-show settings. It wouldn't hurt to click Preview one more time to be sure everything is set up the way you want, but that's up to you. Ready? Click Burn in the Ready To Burn Disc dialog box. Depending upon the length of the items you have chosen to burn, this process could take a few minutes. Wait to be sure you have the proper disc inserted—if not, an error message will appear. But if you have inserted a recordable DVD, you should see a Burning dialog box that shows a status bar as it encodes your information to the disc. Have another cup of coffee or soda, and come back in a few minutes to grab your DVD.

## MAKE MULTIPLE COPIES OF YOUR DVD

If you want to make additional copies of your DVD, *you need to remove the completed DVD and insert a new recordable DVD* before clicking Make Another Copy Of This Disc in the Your Disc Is Ready dialog box.

# Publish Your Movie to the Web

**30 minutes or less**

Now that you are an expert at making movies, you no doubt want everyone to see them. After all, why spend time creating something fabulous if you're the only one who will see it? One good way to let others see your movie and avoid clogging e-mail inboxes is to publish your movie to a Web site.

Doing this has some requirements and limitations, but it's not as hard as you might think. First, you need to have a Web site. You can't just run around publishing your movies to any old Web site (although YouTube is certainly the exception). Then, you must be certain the content in your video is legally owned by you. If you have used video or pictures taken by someone else, you risk running afoul of copyright laws. It's one thing to use those clips personally (although you really shouldn't), but it's quite another to post your thievery publicly.

Also, consider the size and file name of your movie. A file larger than 100KB can often take a long time to download, which means people will get bored and not bother to wait for it. File names on the Web are case-sensitive, so be sure your Web site's Hypertext Markup Language (HTML) code for the movie matches the file name exactly, or no one will be able to download it.

Before you can publish your movie to the Web, you need to publish the movie to your computer. This ensures you can share the movie in any way you like.

### PUBLISH A MOVIE TO YOUR COMPUTER

To publish a movie to your computer, follow these steps:

1. In Movie Maker, click File.

2. Click Publish Movie.

3. Click This Computer.

4. Click Next.

5. Type a name for the movie in the File Name box, and in the Publish To box, select the location where you want the movie saved.

6. Click Next.

7. Choose the settings you want for your movie. These determine the quality and size of your published movie—if your movie is a long one, you may need to readjust these so the size doesn't exceed 4GB, which is a file size limit imposed by the FAT32 file system. Click Publish.

8. We recommend you watch the movie once it's published, so select Play Movie When I Finish.

9. Click Finish.

Now your movie is ready to publish to the Web.

## SET WEB PUBLISHING OPTIONS

You can publish your movie to the Web in many ways. The decision for where to publish depends on what you want to accomplish. If you are an independent film-maker, you can pay to have your movies posted on iFilm, a promotional and marketing tool for independent moviemakers. If you just want to share a video of your child on Halloween with family members, you can use your private Web page.

Many sites are eagerly looking for your video, such as YouTube (shown in Figure 10-4), Google, Yahoo, and more. One nice benefit to using these sites is that you can upload your video for free and just place a link to it in an e-mail or on your own Web site. This saves room on your Web site and makes it easier for others to just click a link to watch your movie. On the flip side, these sites are public—anyone can see your video, so think twice about the content involved before you use a public site.

**Figure 10-4:** Several sites, such as YouTube, let you upload your movies for free.

Here are some popular options for you to consider:

**Google Video**   Lets you upload videos for free and in any length or size. You do need to establish a Google account to take advantage of the service, and a Google video player is required for viewing. *http://video.google.com/video_about.html*

**Yahoo Video**   Lets you upload videos online for free but requires registration and places a 100MB limit on size. *http://video.yahoo.com/*

**YouTube**   Another free online video streaming service. Everything is free, registration is required, and the site has a 100MB/10-minute length limit. *www.youtube.com/*

**Ourmedia**   Yet another option that lets you publish movies on the Web. It's a little more difficult to use than the other three mentioned (registration is required on two separate places, for example, and you must download special software to upload files), but it still serves the same purpose as the others. *www.ourmedia.org/*

You'll find dozens of services like these on the Web; just poke around to see which one you like best. So many options exist today to let you share your movies that it would be a shame not to take advantage of the services these kinds of sites offer.

These two projects are just the tip of the iceberg of what can be done using Windows Vista. A little imagination combined with the applications of Windows Vista can take you a long way toward becoming the geek you knew you always could be. Think of a project you always wished you could do on your computer—chances are good that you have the ability to do it now. Use the Help and Support function if you need to; it has great tips for working through almost anything in Windows Vista. Now put on that geek hat and start innovating!

# PART V Media Center

- Use Windows Media Center
- Access and organize media
- Explore and optimize Media Center views
- Watch your library folders
- Optimize Media Center
- Expand Media Center with a media extender

# **Bring** It All Together with Media Center

# CHAPTER 11

If you've ever wanted to be a complete couch potato and run all your media from one remote control while eating bonbons on a pile of pillows, get ready to lie down. In just a couple of well-spent hours, you too can be a media mogul and run your entertainment empire with the flick of a finger. You'll need to get organized and become proficient with Windows Media Center, and depending on which tasks you decide to tackle, you could be done in less time than it takes to clean out the closet—you know, the one everyone is afraid to open for fear of falling objects and a subsequent hospital visit? Yeah, that one. Who wants to clean closets anyway? It's far more fun to play on the computer!

# Navigate the Windows Media Center Interface

**15 minutes**

Windows Media Center is a simple way of controlling all your media from your PC; from one location, you can access songs, photos, TV shows, and even your Xbox 360. The Windows Vista operating system offers support for digital and high-definition cable TV and an easy-to-use menu system plus multiroom access so you can enjoy the media stored on your PC from just about anywhere in your home. It can all take place via remote control and works with the following Windows Vista accessibility features: Narrator, Magnifier, and Descriptive Video Services (DVS). If you have a rack of home theater equipment, get ready for a garage sale—you aren't going to need most of it.

*In just a couple of well-spent hours, you too can be a media mogul and run your entertainment empire with the flick of a finger.*

> **NOTE** You will need a wired or wireless home network to take advantage of some aspects of Media Center, and you need to have Windows Vista Ultimate or Vista Ultimate Home Premium on a computer with Media Center.

One feature of Media Center we love is how simple it is to find and enjoy the media you want. The interface is so visual that it's easy to identify where you want to go. Thumbnail pictures on the computer or TV screen, for example, let you quickly find that CD or picture or TV show you want to look at—you can even view those thumbnails while watching a movie or something else on the screen.

The menu system—shown in Figure 11-1—is almost simple enough to use without instruction. Notice we said "almost," so spend a little time just playing around with it to get the hang of how it scrolls and how it opens commands. You can use the Microsoft Windows Button at any time to return to the Start screen.

**Figure 11-1:** The menu system in Media Center follows the overall Windows Vista concept of visual simplicity.

On the Start screen, you'll see a vertical menu in the center section of the screen and horizontal menus that correspond to each section of the vertical menu. This layout repeats throughout Media Center, by the way. Arrows appear if additional menu choices are available but not shown on your screen. Just click an arrow to move through a menu, or click a command to begin a task or operation. Table 11-1 shows you which commands correspond to the vertical menu options. Additional commands become available once you have selected a horizontal command.

Also notice the menu thumbnails. Every piece of the menu is divided into categories, with thumbnails that let you easily see and access what you want within each category. Rest your pointer on a thumbnail, and watch how individual thumbnails enlarge for easier viewing. Click a thumbnail, and the program will start. Let's begin!

| VERTICAL MENU SECTION | CORRESPONDING COMMANDS |
|---|---|
| TV + Movies | Recorded TV, Set Up TV |
| Online Media | Program Library |
| Tasks | Settings, Shutdown, Add Extender, Media Only |
| Music | Music Library, Play All, Radio, Search |
| Pictures + Videos | Picture Library, Play All, Video Library |

**Table 11-1:** Menus and commands

# Access and Organize Media

**1 hour**

With Media Center, you'll first want to make sure your files are organized and easy to access. Depending upon the number of files you have, this process could take you less or more than an hour, but the basic process is really pretty simple: Figure out where the media is that you will want to access (music, videos, pictures, recorded TV programs, games, and so on), and be sure to tell Media Center where that media is located. Media Center will do the rest for you by organizing those files into one of its libraries for easy access. For example, Figure 11-2 shows a music library.

**Figure 11-2:** Media Center libraries can keep track of all your media, no matter where it's located.

## STORE YOUR FILES

Media Center files can come from just about anywhere on your computer or network, but Media Center automatically draws from a few key places when it goes looking for your files: the Music, Pictures, Videos, and Public folders. You can also tell it to access other folders you designate—we outline how later in this chapter. Remember, though, the more places you store files, the harder it is for you to find them later if you are *not* in Media Center!

When you download files to your computer or network, you can use any of the previously mentioned folders, or you can create new ones—just remember to tell Media Center where to look for your files. As you store them, give them names that will help you easily remember what they are—"movie1" isn't a good title, for example, if your video library will eventually have hundreds of movies. You can give pictures easy tags—simple names such as Forest Flowers—so you can easily find them by name; they will display a date for easy reference as well.

## UNDERSTAND YOUR LIBRARIES

You have four libraries within Media Center to choose from when you are searching for media:

- Picture library
- Video library
- Music library
- Program library

Each library holds relevant files, which makes it easy for you to scroll through and find what you are looking for on the Start screen. Media Center automatically places files into a library based on its file type.

## VIEW THE FILE TYPES SUPPORTED BY MEDIA CENTER

As you get used to Media Center, you'll realize quickly that you want to make it the default player for your video, music, and picture files. The following sections list the basic file types that Media Center supports; more are available if you install new codecs (compression hardware or software).

### MUSIC FILE TYPES AND EXTENSIONS

- Audio CDS: .cda
- Windows Media Audio file: .asx, .wm, .wma, .wmx
- Windows Audio file: .wav

### VIDEO FILE TYPES AND EXTENSIONS

- Windows Media file: .wm and .asf
- Windows Media Video file: .wmv
- Windows video file: .avi
- Movie file: .mpeg, .mpg, .mpe, .m1v, .mp2, .mpv2

### PICTURE FILE TYPES AND EXTENSIONS

- Joint Photographic Experts Group: .jpg, .jpeg
- Tagged Image File Format: .tif, .tiff
- Graphics Interchange Format: .gif
- Bitmap: .bmp
- Windows Metafile: .wmf
- Portable Network Graphics: .png

# Explore and Optimize Media Center Views

 **20 minutes**

As you work with different areas of the interface, you will notice that you can make the thumbnails larger or smaller. You can perform other tasks with Media Center views too, such as showing taskbar notifications (in the Startup And Window Behavior, Settings menu) and changing color schemes or video background colors (in the Visual And Sound Effects, Settings menu).

Here are a few more views to consider customizing:

**Pictures**   Click Settings, and click Pictures. This is where you can choose whether to show pictures in random order, in subfolders, and with captions. You can also choose when and where to show song information during a slide show.

**Visualization**   Also under Settings, you can access this by clicking Music. With this option, you can choose which visualizations (geometric shapes, splashes of color, and so on) to watch as songs play.

**TV closed captioning**   Click Settings, click TV, and then click Closed Captioning to set closed captioning options. The options are On When Muted, On, and Off.

# Set Up Library Folder Watch

 **10 minutes**

Another great feature of Media Center is its ability to keep an eye on your Music, Pictures, and Videos folders for media files. You can also designate other folders for Media Center to watch—or tell it to stop watching certain folders. This lets Media Center automatically add your new files so you can enjoy them once they have been downloaded. On the Start screen, scroll to Tasks, and click Settings. Then perform the following steps depending on whether you want to add or remove folders from the watch list.

## ADD FOLDERS TO WATCH

To add folders to the watch list, follow these steps:

1. Click Library Setup.

2. Select Add Folder To Watch, as shown in Figure 11-3. Click Next.

3. Select which folders you want to add at the prompt, and click Next.

   Options are Add Folders On This Computer, Add Shared Folders From Another Computer, or Add Folders From Both Locations.

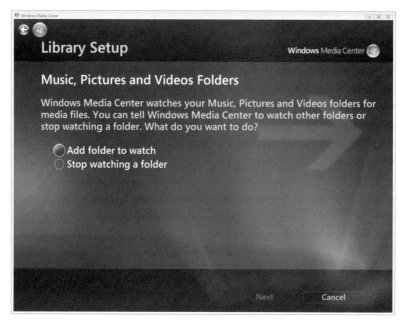

Figure 11-3: Media Center watches your folders for media files.

④ Select the folder that contains the media. Click Next.

⑤ Verify the location you have chosen on the Add Folders screen. Click Finish if it is correct.

⑥ The Adding Media window appears, asking whether you want to wait while the media is added. If you want to wait, do nothing. If you want to do something else in Media Center, click OK.

⑦ If you need to change the location, click Back, and reselect the folder location.

## STOP WATCHING FOLDERS

To stop watching folders, follow these steps:

① Click Library Setup.

② Select Stop Watching A Folder. Click Next.

③ Select which folders you want to stop watching by clearing check boxes at the prompt, and then click Next.

④ Select the folder location that contains media. Click Next.

⑤ Verify the location you have chosen to stop watching on the Stop Watching Folders screen. Click Finish if it is correct.

⑥ If you need to change the location, click Back, and reselect the folder location.

# Optimize Media Center

**5 minutes**

To keep your computer running smoothly, you really should establish an optimization schedule for Media Center. *Optimization* is just a fancy word for freeing up some computer brainpower so it can think more effectively and respond more quickly to your requests. You can set up Media Center to perform optimization tasks automatically through the Settings screen, as shown in Figure 11-4.

**Figure 11-4:** Establishing an optimization schedule in Media Center helps your media respond more quickly to your requests.

### SET UP A MEDIA CENTER OPTIMIZATION SCHEDULE

To set up a Media Center optimization schedule, follow these steps:

1. On the Start menu, scroll to Tasks. Click Settings.

2. Click General.

3. Click Optimization.

4. Select Perform Optimization.

5. In Optimization Schedule, type the time of day you want the optimization tasks to run.

6. Click Save.

> **NOTE** You cannot use Media Center or Media Center extenders while optimization tasks are running. (See the next section for more information about media extenders.)

## Expand Media Center with a Media Extender

 1 hour

Are you sitting in your favorite TV-watching chair? A *media extender* is a separate external component that extends Media Center to your entertainment center, letting you take advantage of Media Center features from the comfort of your living room chair. Your computer stays in the office or kitchen or wherever, and you access Media Center through the entertainment center. You can add up to five TVs by using media extenders. Another bonus? You can watch and pause live TV shows or record them digitally for later viewing...all together now, let's say, "I don't need TiVo if I have a media extender!"

As mentioned earlier, however, this is the piece of Media Center that needs a wired or wireless home network and Windows Vista Ultimate or Windows Vista Home Premium on a computer with Media Center.

To use the media extender once it's installed, you simply use an on-screen menu via a remote control. The hardest part of all this is going to be getting off the couch and purchasing the media extender. You can use a variety of devices as media extenders—including Xbox 360, as shown in Figure 11-5. You can find media extenders at major retail outlets, and they typically sell for about $200. Just ask your helpful computer salesperson for help, whip out the credit card, and head back home to follow the steps in the next sections.

**Figure 11-5:** Xbox 360 works great as a media extender for Media Center.

## ADD A MEDIA EXTENDER

To add a Media Extender to your home network, you need to connect it to your computer and log on to Windows Vista. Verify that your computer is connected to your home network. Then follow these steps:

1. Turn on your extender, and verify it is connected to your home network.

2. Note the setup key for your extender that appears on the TV or monitor—it's best to write it down.

3. In the Media Center Start screen, scroll to Tasks, and click Add Extender.

4. Click Next on the Welcome to Windows Media Center Extender Setup screen.

5. Use your remote control or keyboard to type the eight-digit setup key on the Enter The Setup Key screen. Click Next.

6. Follow the steps in Extender Setup.

7. Click Finish.

## TAKING NOTE OF MEDIA EXTENDER AUTOMATIC CHANGES

After you set up the extender, Windows Vista will make changes to the Windows Firewall exceptions list and Windows Firewall settings. You will notice the Windows Media Center Extender service (mcx2svc) start on your computer—along with other dependent services—when this happens.

## ADD XBOX 360 TO MEDIA CENTER

 **25 minutes**

Xbox 360 has Media Center extender technology built right into it—if you have one of these, you can use it to connect to the Media Center music library by pressing the green button on the remote control. Just select My Music from the menu, and start dancing (or humming—whatever you prefer). But first, you have to add your Xbox 360 to your PC. Xbox Live Connectivity is required to connect to the Windows Vista–based PC. Test your live connection on your Xbox 360 console, then go to Media, and select Windows Media Center. Now follow these steps:

1. Advance through the on-screen instructions, and write down the eight-digit Media Center setup key.

2. On your Windows Vista–based PC, set Network Category to Private.

   You perform this step through the Control Panel: Click Network And Internet, and then go to Network Center. Select Switch Category until it says Private Network.

3. Start Media Center. On the Start screen, scroll to Tasks, and click Add Extender.

4. Follow the on-screen instructions.

Windows Vista is not compatible with the original Xbox.

In this chapter, you learned how to navigate Media Center by using the horizontal and vertical menu selections and commands. By now, your media should be organized in folders easy for Media Center to monitor, which will make accessing your media fast and simple. We discussed Media Center views, how to set up or remove library folder watches, and how to establish an optimization schedule. And, if you want Media Center throughout your home, we explained the concept of media extenders and how to set one up. Finished with those bonbons yet?

- **Burn a CD**

- **Burn a DVD**

- **Create a DVD slide show of pictures with background music**

- **Listen to free online music and radio stations**

- **Explore remote control options**

- **Command Media Center with your voice**

# **Have** Fun with Media Center

# CHAPTER 12

There's no point in having Windows Media Center if you can't have a little fun with it, right? And there are so many different ways to have that fun! For us, fun often involves music and pictures—and when they are in combination, it's even better. For our spouses, fun means using a remote control and speech recognition to run the TV, stereo, computer, and other features of Media Center. Whatever your idea of fun, we're betting you'll have some as you try a few tasks in this chapter. Oh, sure, there's a bit of work to be done, too. But how hard can something be when you can do it in ten minutes?

# Burn a CD

 **10 minutes**

For those of you old enough to remember mix tapes, keep that concept in mind as we talk about burning CDs. For the younger set, Microsoft Zune and the Apple iPod are the modern-day equivalent to mix tapes. Regardless of what you call your collection of music, it's all about being able to access the music you love without having to listen to a lot of tunes you don't like.

*For us, fun often involves music and pictures—and when they are in combination, it's even better.*

Burning a CD means you can select music by individual song, entire album, genre, playlist, or artist and capture it all on one CD for playback. With Windows Media Center, you can burn an audio CD from a variety of formats; the WMA, MP3, and WAV file formats are the most common.

When you pop a recordable CD or DVD into your burner, Windows Media Player or Windows DVD Maker may appear as the default program, as shown in Figure 12-1. You can

**Figure 12-1:** A dialog box from Windows Media Player may appear when you insert a recordable CD into your CD burner. Don't let it distract you!

certainly use these programs to burn your CD or DVD, but in this chapter we will focus on using Media Center as the burn medium. Simply close the other program when it appears, and follow the steps as instructed in each of the following sections.

## BURN AN AUDIO CD

To burn an audio CD, follow these steps:

1. Place a recordable CD into your DVD burner.

2. Go to the Media Center Start screen, scroll to Tasks, and click Burn CD/DVD.

3. Click Audio CD.

4. Click Next.

5. In Name This CD, give your CD a title. Click Next.

6. In Choose Music, select the place where your media is located. Click the media. A check mark will appear to verify the item you have selected.

7. Click Next. On the Review & Edit List, decide whether you need to rename the DVD, clear your selections, or add more items.

8. Click Burn DVD. When the Initiating Copy dialog box appears, click Yes. The process may take quite some time, depending on the files you have selected. Click OK if you want to do other tasks while the disc is being burned.

9. When the Completing Disc Creation notification appears, click Done.

# Burn a DVD

**10 minutes**

When you make movies, it's always fun to share them with others. You can burn DVDs of your movies and other digital data without leaving Media Center. You have two ways to burn a DVD: as a video DVD and as a data DVD.

With video DVDs, Media Center converts the video files you select to a video format recognized by standard DVD players for easy playback. You can usually play these video DVDs on your computer, too.

With data DVDs, nothing is converted—files are merely copied from your computer to your DVD, so the original format stays intact. Data DVDs can store a lot of files, but because there is no conversion involved, some DVD players and computers might not be able to play them. Data DVDs are best for backing up your digital media files, rather than sharing the data on them with others.

**NOTE** By the way, there are also data and audio CDs, too. Files conversions work the same way on them as they do on the different types of DVDs.

# RECORDING TIPS

You can record approximately 120 minutes of video on a single-sided, single-layer DVD and 220 minutes on a single-sided, double-layer DVD. We say "approximately" because the actual time will vary depending upon your computer's DVD burner speed, your available system resources, and other factors.

If a digital media file is copyright protected, it often cannot be played on computers beyond the original. Pay attention to the media usage rights when you download a file—they will tell you how you can use the file and whether the rights expire after a certain time limit. It's not just TV shows that have these limitations.

The length of time it will take to actually burn a DVD will vary according to the content being burned. We've estimated about 10 minutes for your first try at this with a simple file; once you get the hang of it, you'll be able to set the process up and perform other tasks while the computer does the rest of the work for you.

## BURN A TV SHOW OR VIDEO TO A DVD

To burn a TV show or video to a DVD, follow these steps:

1. Place a recordable DVD into your DVD burner.
2. Go to the Media Center Start screen, scroll to Tasks, and click Burn CD/DVD.
3. Click Video DVD.
4. Click Next.
5. In Name This DVD, give your DVD a title. Click Next.
6. Select the place where your media is located. Click Next.
7. Click the media. A check mark will appear to verify the item you have selected. If you want to add more media, you need to click Add More.

   Repeat steps 6 and 7 until you have all the items you want.

8. Click Next. On the Review & Edit List, decide whether you need to rename the DVD, clear your selections, or add more items.

⑨ Click Burn DVD. When the Initiating Copy dialog box appears, click Yes. The process may take quite some time, depending on the files you have selected, as shown in Figure 12-2. Click OK if you want to do other tasks while the disc is being burned.

⑩ When the Completing Disc Creation notification appears, click Done.

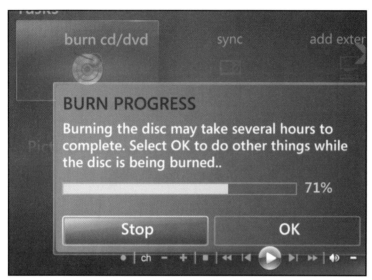

Figure 12-2: Burning a DVD can take some time depending on what you're adding to the DVD. Media Center lets you do other tasks while it works.

## BURN MUSIC, PICTURES, OR VIDEOS TO A DATA DVD

These steps for burning a data DVD are almost identical to the previous steps for burning TV shows or videos to a video DVD. The only difference is that you click Data DVD instead of Video DVD. Follow the steps outlined in the previous section, and make that change.

NOTE Slide shows burned to DVDs in Media Center are encoded as MPEG-2 video files, with any audio files you select encoded as Dolby Digital audio. This means the pictures will display as the music plays. Cool, huh?

# Create a DVD Slide Show with Background Music

 **10 minutes**

You can create a DVD slide show in two ways: with and without music. Let's face it, slide shows can be boring when you're just looking at pictures slipping by. So why not add a little pizzazz to all those pictures you're burning onto that DVD? A bit of music could sure spice up the mood and add some context or fun to the slide show.

If you decide to do this, you should remember a couple of points. First, pictures you add to the DVD will play at seven-second intervals. They will also play in whatever order you add them to the DVD, so think carefully as you add pictures. In addition, music will play in the order you add it to the DVD—just like the pictures do. You'll have a chance to make edits as you go, but once you click Burn DVD, there are no second chances!

To create your DVD slide show with background music, follow these steps:

1. Place a recordable DVD into your DVD burner.

2. Go to the Media Center Start screen, scroll to Tasks, and click Burn CD/DVD.

3. Click DVD Slide Show.

4. Click Next.

5. In Name This DVD, give your DVD a title. Click Next.

6. Select the place where your media is located. Click Next.

7. Make your music selection in Choose Music by scrolling through the options. If you want to add more media, you need to click Add More.

   Repeat steps 6 and 7 until you have all the items you want.

> **NOTE** You will be prompted to choose both music and pictures if you have selected only one type of media. If you did not mean to create a slide show with music, click Cancel, and start over again, selecting Burn Video or Data DVD instead.

⑧ Click Next. On the Review & Edit List, decide whether you need to rename the DVD, clear your selections, or add more items.

⑨ Click Burn DVD. When the Initiating Copy dialog box appears, click Yes. The process may take quite some time, depending on the files you have selected. Click OK if you want to perform other tasks while the disc is being burned.

⑩ When the Completing Disc Creation notification appears, click Done.

# Listen to Free Online Music and Radio Stations

 **20 minutes**

To listen to free online music and radio stations in Media Center, you need an FM radio tuner or an Internet radio partner application installed on your computer (or both). Once those are installed, you can find and listen to FM or Internet radio stations and create presets so you always have them handy. The only reason this might take you 20 minutes or longer is because you'll want to stop and listen to all the stations.

## LISTEN TO FM RADIO WITH MEDIA CENTER

To listen to FM radio with Media Center, follow these steps:

① On the Media Center Start screen, scroll to Music, click Radio, and then click FM Radio.

② You can let Media Center find a station for you by using the Seek and Tune commands, or you can type the numbers of the station by using your numeric keypad.

③ Use the buttons on the bottom of your screen to play music, change channels, pause music, and so on.

## CREATE A PRESET FOR YOUR FM RADIO STATION

To create a preset for your FM radio station, follow these steps:

1. On the Media Center Start screen, scroll to Music, click Radio, and then click FM Radio.

2. Click Seek or click Tune to find the station you want, as shown in Figure 12-3. Click Save As Preset.

3. Type the name of the station, and click Save.

Figure 12-3: You can listen to both Internet and FM radio with Media Center.

## LISTEN TO INTERNET RADIO WITH MEDIA CENTER

To listen to Internet radio with Media Center, follow these steps:

1. On the Media Center Start screen, scroll to Online Media, and click Browse Categories.

2. Click Music & Radio.

3. Click the online radio station you want to listen to, and start jammin'!

**NOTE** You can also listen to Internet radio and download music with Windows Media Player. Go to the Media Guide, and click Internet Radio for hundreds of radio station choices.

# Explore Remote Control Options

 **20 minutes**

Frankly, we don't think there is much point to hopping up and down to change settings or options in Media Center. Therefore, we highly recommend using a remote control (unless you prefer speech recognition as explained in the next section). You'll need to obtain the remote control from a local computer store; it will have a variety of options from which to choose. You also need an infrared receiver (IR) or a transceiver—you can connect this device with a USB cable or through Bluetooth or radio frequency. Ask the computer store salesperson to help you determine what will work best with your computer system.

Once you have the remote control set up, you can do almost anything you need to with Media Center. Every remote control approved for Media Center has a set of required buttons; but some buttons may not be needed if your computer does not have TV tuner hardware. The required buttons are as follows:

**Navigation buttons**   The green Start button plus Up, Down, Left, Right, OK, More, and Back

**Transport controls**   Play/Pause, Play, Pause, Stop, Rewind, Fast Forward, Skip Forward, Skip Backward

**Audio and video controls**   Power/Standby, Power On, Power Off, Volume Up, Volume Down Off, Mute, Channel/Page Up, Channel/Page Down

**Media Center shortcut keys**   Guide

**Teletext**   Red, Green, Blue, Yellow, Teletext On/Off

The More button is definitely one to get to know well. Pressing it displays a list of additional options depending on what you have selected on the screen. It also lets you access the Settings screen from anywhere in Media Center.

You can also put your Media Center computer into Sleep mode with a remote (now there's a nice feature late at night!). If a show needs to be recorded, no worries. Your computer can determine that and pops back on when required.

# **Command** Media **Center with Your Voice**

 **1 hour**

Did you know you can use your voice to control Media Center? You can use Windows Speech Recognition for other tasks too, but it's by far the most entertaining to lie on your couch and speak your commands as you gobble those bonbons. With Windows Speech Recognition, you can run programs and interact with Windows by speaking common commands.

You need to have a microphone hooked up to your computer, and you need to take care of some basics such as creating a voice profile so the computer recognizes and understands your voice. We suggest you get a top-of-the-line microphone if you plan on being halfway across the room while commanding your Media Center—speech recognition deteriorates in direct correlation to the quality of your microphone! Headsets are a good idea if you plan on wandering around the house.

Once you have set up your microphone (go to Control Panel, Speech Recognition Options), it's time to take the tutorial and train your computer to recognize your speech. Both of these are also located in the Control Panel under Speech Recognition Options. We're not going to give you step-by-step instructions here; those are easily available with wizards in the tutorial and training sections of Control Panel, as we just mentioned. But to give you an idea of how this could easily work for Media Center, Table 12-1 shows examples of the commonly used commands in Windows Speech Recognition and how you would say them. Give yourself at least an hour to practice with this cool feature, and then play to your heart's content—all while in the prone position, of course.

| FOR THIS TYPE OF COMMAND... | YOU JUST SAY THIS... |
| --- | --- |
| Clicking a menu command | "Click *File*." |
| | "Click *Computer*." |
| Double-clicking a menu command | "Double-click *File*." |
| | "Double-click *Computer*." |
| Switching to an open program | "Switch to *Media Center*." (Use the name of the program.) |
| Scrolling | "Scroll *up*." (You can also say *down, left,* and *right*.) |
| Showing a list of applicable commands. | "What can I say?" |
| Making the computer start or stop listening to you | "Start listening." |
| | "Stop listening." |
| Minimizing all the windows so you can see your desktop | "Show desktop." |
| Clicking something you don't know the name of. | "Show numbers." (Numbers will appear for every item in the active window.) |
| Undoing | "Undo." |

Table 12-1: Windows Speech Recognition commands

*You can replace items in italics with different words for equally useful results.*

In this chapter, we showed you how to burn DVDs and CDs, as well as how to create a DVD slide show with background music. You also learned how to access free online music and FM radio stations, explored using a remote control with Media Center, and took a crash course in commanding Media Center with your voice (you really need to try the last two!).

- **Watch live TV**
- **Record your favorite TV programs**
- **Manage your saved TV programs**
- **Rent and download movies**
- **Set parental controls**

# **Play** with TV

# CHAPTER 13

Oh, boy. Now we're getting into the *real* reason you wanted Windows Media Center, aren't we? Media Center lets you record your TV shows so you don't need to spend all that money on TiVo. And you can do even more with the TV features, too. Let's make something clear, however. You can't use Media Center with your television if your computer does not have a TV tuner. So before you get too excited, run out and get one if you don't already have one.

Once you have that tuner installed, find your couch potato hat. You'll need it. And maybe a couch potato blanket, too, to keep you warm and cozy as you use your remote control or speech recognition to their fullest potentials.

# Watch Live TV

*Media Center lets you record your TV shows so you don't need to spend all that money on TiVo.*

Using Windows Media Center to record live TV and movies is our favorite feature. Oh, sure, we use the other features too, but when we can watch what we want when we want to, that's when we're the happiest. We'll cover several basic topics in this section: watch, rewind, pause, and fast/skip forward. Why will this take you two minutes to perform most of the time? Well, it's an overestimate, frankly; we wanted to give you enough time to choose the program you want to watch. The actual commands and steps take just seconds.

Media Center offers a *guide*, which is a great way to find the TV shows you want to watch. It's like *TV Guide*, only better and on the screen in front of you. Programs appear in a table with the date, time, program title, channel name, and channel number. You can navigate the guide by using your remote control or by using your mouse.

### ENJOY LIVE TV

 **2 minutes**

You can start watching live TV in one of three ways: by going to the Start screen (scroll to TV + Movies, and click Live TV), by using your remote control (press Live TV), or by going to the guide (go to the Start screen, scroll to TV + Movies, and click Guide). Then, follow these steps for different viewing options:

1. Change the channel by moving the mouse and clicking the channel up or down button on the screen.

2. Display information about the program by right-clicking the TV show on the screen and then clicking Program Info. (Click Watch to return to the show.)

3. Go to the last channel you watched by pressing the Enter button on the remote control.

## PAUSE, REWIND, FAST-FORWARD, OR SKIP FORWARD DURING LIVE TV

**1 minute**

Did you miss something a character said? No worries—pause the program by moving the mouse and clicking Pause on the screen or by pressing Pause on your remote. Move the mouse again, and click Rewind (or use your remote's Rewind button). If you prefer to fast-forward or skip forward, simply make that selection instead of Rewind.

# Record Your Favorite TV Programs

Recording a live television show or movie is incredibly simple, and you can do it in a couple of different ways. But remember, programs begin recording when you direct them to start recording. You can't record an entire show if you jump in halfway through it and start recording. That's just common sense, of course, but we thought it was important enough to stress.

Before you start recording a program, you should set some general recording options. These will let you specify how long to keep a recorded show, for example, or when a show should start or stop recording. Once you set up your general recording options, recording an actual show will take only seconds. We say five minutes just to give you time to figure out which shows you want to record and select the general options you want. Figure 13-1 shows you an example of a recorded TV program.

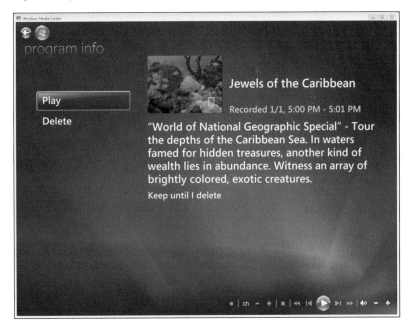

**Figure 13-1:** Recording TV programs means you can watch any program at any time you want.

## SET GENERAL RECORDING OPTIONS

 **5 minutes**

To set general recording options, follow these steps:

**1** On the Media Center Start screen, scroll to Tasks, and click Settings.

**2** Click TV.

**3** Click Recorder.

**4** Click Recording Defaults.

- In Keep, click – or + to specify how long you want to keep the recorded TV show.

- In Quality, click – or + to select the quality you want the show recorded in.

- In Start When Possible, indicate the time the program should start recording.

- In Stop When Possible, indicate the time the program should stop recording.

- In Preferred Audio Language, click English or Any Other Language.

- In Series Only Recording Defaults, specify how many recordings of the show you want to keep if you are recording any television series.

**5** Click Save.

Now you're ready to begin recording your programs. Choose one of the following options to get started.

## UNDERSTAND THE TWO PRIMARY WAYS TO RECORD A TV SHOW OR MOVIE

You can record TV shows and movies either while the program is playing or by setting up the recording in advance, which is most often done with a weekly TV series.

## RECORD WHILE A PROGRAM IS PLAYING

**1 minute**

To record while the program is playing, do one of the following:

- Choose the program you want to watch by selecting the show in the guide or by using the Search function. Press Record on the remote control, or click Record on the screen when the show starts.

- Tune your television to the program. Move the mouse, and then press Record on the remote.

To set up recording before a program begins playing, follow these steps:

**1** On the Media Center Start screen, scroll to TV + Movies, and click Guide.

**2** Locate the program you want, and right-click it.

**3** Click Record.

## RECORD A WEEKLY TV SERIES

**1 minute**

To record a weekly TV series, follow these steps:

**1** On the Media Center Start screen, scroll to TV + Movies, and click Guide.

**2** Locate the series you want, and right-click it.

**3** Click Record Series.

# RECORD WITH KEYWORDS

Everyone has a favorite actor, director, or even topic they enjoy. Rather than scan television guides for specific programs and playing times, Media Center lets you record TV programs based on keywords. Yep—pick an actor or director's name, a movie or program title, or just a generic keyword, and when a program airs that matches your keyword, it will be recorded. Ahhhhh. Now we can find Elvis whenever we want without lifting a finger after the initial setup. Life just doesn't get any better than that!

*continued*

**2 minutes**

To record by keyword, follow these steps:

1. On the Media Center Start screen, scroll to TV + Movies, and click Recorded TV.

2. Click Add Recording.

3. Click Keyword.

4. Click Actor Name, Director Name, Movie Title, Program Title, or Generic Keyword depending on how you want Media Center to find your program.

5. Type a keyword for your recording, and then click the matching keyword in the resulting list.

6. Click – or + for the different settings to specify the criteria for your custom recording.

7. Click Record.

8. Click OK.

# Manage Your Recorded TV Programs

Once you have recorded a few television programs, you may start running into a few issues you hadn't considered. Maybe your recordings are starting 30 seconds after a program begins or you're running out of space on your hard disk. The following are some tips to help you manage your recorded TV programs so you don't miss a critical moment or even an entire episode because of recording issues.

### DELETE, DELETE, DELETE!

Get rid of the programs you have recorded but haven't found time to watch. You know which ones these are—you've recorded 32 episodes of *Friends* in three weeks but have watched only six. Or maybe you no longer need that Oprah segment about dieting since you've already lost ten pounds. Whatever—just delete the programs you aren't really watching. They are just taking up space on your hard disk and could prevent Media Center from recording newer, more interesting shows because of space limitations.

You have two ways to delete a program:

- Change the Keep option.

- Delete a program manually.

## CHANGE THE KEEP OPTION TO DELETE A RECORDED PROGRAM

**1.5 minutes**

To change the Keep option to delete a recorded program, follow these steps:

1. Go to the Media Center Start screen, and scroll to Tasks.

2. Click Settings.

3. Click TV.

4. Click Recorder.

5. Click Recording Defaults.

6. Choose the Keep option that works best for you:

   - Until Space Needed

   - For 1 Week

   - Until I Watch

   - Until I Delete

**TROUBLESHOOTING** If you find that some programs aren't being recorded— yet you know you set them to record—verify whether they have been marked Until I Delete or Until I Watch. If you marked one of these, your computer prob- ably has run out of disk space to record new programs until you watch or delete an old one. Clean out the old programs you aren't going to watch so Media Center has enough room to record the new stuff, or consider changing some programs options to Until Space Needed or For 1 Week.

### DELETE A RECORDED PROGRAM MANUALLY

 **1.5 minutes**

To delete a recorded program manually, follow these steps:

1. Go to the Media Center Start screen, and scroll to TV + Movies.

2. Click Recorded TV.

3. Click the program you want deleted.

4. Click Delete on the Program Info screen.

5. Click Yes.

### VERIFY OPTIONS

You should verify that your recording times are set properly in Set General Options. You should also verify your computer's clock at this time—if your recordings are missing part of a program, chances are good your clock and the television's clock are different.

While you're verifying options, ask yourself whether you're happy with the quality of the recordings you're seeing. If not, you can adjust those settings under Quality.

## Download Movies

It's time to get rid of your Blockbuster card or Netflix account. Instead, why not rent and download movies through Media Center from the comfort of your couch? Several partners work directly with Media Center to let you download movies through the Program Library in Online Media. Some may require installation, such as Kazaa or CinemaNow—if you see No Services or a similar message when you access your program library in Online Media, you do not have any partner programs installed and will need to obtain one before you can download movies.

It's important to remember that there is always a risk that a file you download could contain a virus or other malicious software. Be sure your antivirus software is up-to-date before you download anything from the Internet. Once you've rented or downloaded a movie, you can access it through the program library in Online Media.

## A WORD ABOUT ONLINE STORES

We mentioned Kazaa and CinemaNow (shown in Figure 13-2) already; both are great online stores with lots of movies and other media to buy or rent. You'll find plenty of other stores on the Web too. These stores are subscription based, and each has agreements with different movie studios, so you'll find varying selection at each site. Typically, the site will offer you a range of options: You can buy a video and download it directly to your computer for watching through Media Center, you can buy a video to burn to DVD, you can rent a movie, or you can watch a free movie instantly on the screen (but it doesn't download to your computer).

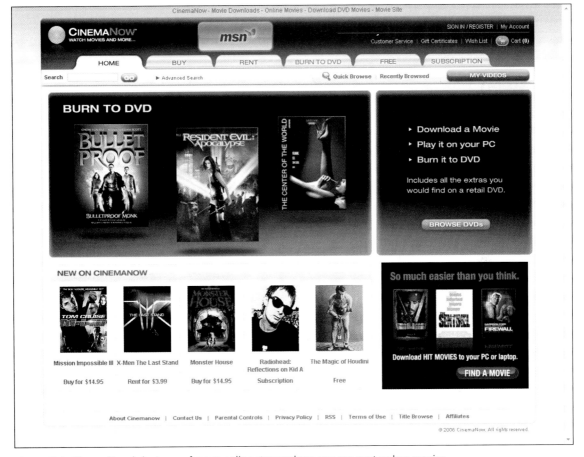

**Figure 13-2:** CinemaNow is just one of many online stores where you can rent or buy movies.

The reason for all these options has to do with the licensing agreements for different movies. If you buy a movie, don't assume you will be able to automatically burn it to DVD—special security protections often prevent this if the licensing agreement doesn't allow it.

Movies take approximately one hour to one-and-a-half hours to download on a high-speed connection, and you will need about 1.5GB of free space for each one. Prices range from as little as $.49 US for a rental with limited viewings to as much as $19.99 US for a straight download you can keep forever.

**NOTE** You can also listen to Internet radio and download music with Windows Media Player 11. Go to the media guide, and click Internet Radio for hundreds of radio station choices.

# Set Parental Controls

If you have kids, then you know how hard it is to keep track of them. A handy Media Center feature for parents is Parental Controls. When you activate it, the kids can watch only the TV and movie content that you deem appropriate. You can block all rated programs, programs for a general audience, programs requiring parental guidance, and even programs intended for adults. You can also set ratings for fantasy violence, suggestive language, offensive language, sexual content, and violence.

 **5 minutes**

To set parental controls, follow these steps:

❶ On the Media Center Start screen, scroll to Tasks, and click Settings.

❷ Click General.

❸ Click Parental Controls. You will be asked to type a four-digit number to set your code.

④ Do one of the following:

- To set Parental Controls for TV programs, click TV Ratings, and then select Turn On TV Blocking, as shown in Figure 13-3. Make your selection for the rating. Note that selecting Block Unrated TV Programs will restrict content that is not rated. Click Advanced to adjust the ratings settings for more control.

- To set Parental Controls for DVDs and movies, click Movie/DVD Ratings, and then select Turn On TV Blocking. Selecting Block Unrated TV Movies will control content that is not rated.

⑤ Click Save.

NOTE Media Center uses ratings from the TV broadcast signal to determine which shows can be watched—this sometimes results in a program being played that you thought was blocked. This happens because the rating listed in the guide differs from the TV signal. There are lots of reasons for this mismatch, but it doesn't occur often.

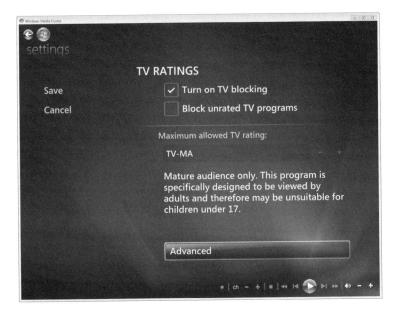

Figure 13-3: With parental controls, you can block programs according to your family's needs.

So, now you are a Media Center pro, right? You know how to watch live TV as well as record and manage your programs, you can rent or buy online movies, and you can block the kids from programs they have no business watching. It's time to move on then.

# PART VI Everyday Living

- Organize your life by using Windows Calendar

- Let Windows Sidebar be your second set of eyes

- Play games by using Windows Vista and Media Center

- Restrict what your children can access

- Protect your investment with Windows Defender

- Interact with friends with Windows Live Messenger

# **Spice Up** Your Life with the New Features of Windows Vista

# CHAPTER 14

You've been learning about all the different programs that come with the Windows Vista operating system, but Windows Vista itself has some pretty cool features beyond those programs that can be pretty entertaining to use. With Windows Vista, you get an integrated calendar, the Windows Sidebar that gives you information at a glance, games, parental controls, defense against intruders (on your computer—not your home! You need an alarm system for that!), speech recognition, and instant messaging. Your everyday life is filled with all kinds of activities, and Windows Vista can help you sort through them so you have plenty of time to spend with family and friends—online or off.

# Use Windows Calendar **to Organize Your Life and Family**

*Your everyday life is filled with all kinds of activities, and Windows Vista can help you sort through them so you have plenty of time to spend with family and friends—online or off.*

If you've ever wished for a single calendar that can help you plan and manage your own activities as well as coordinate the rest of your family's activities, look no further. Windows Calendar is built right into Windows Vista and offers several features you will probably find useful. The Windows Calendar automated integration features make it the easiest calendar we've seen for groups of people to use. You can create appointments, tasks, reminders, and priorities; review and compare multiple calendars; import information from calendar Web sites that use the iCalendar format; publish your own calendar to the Web; and send e-mail appointments and invitations to friends and family directly from your calendar.

That's a lot of organization in one place! Since we don't have all day to get you organized, we'll hit the highlights. First you need to open Windows Calendar. You can do that by clicking the Start menu and typing **Windows Calendar** in the Start Search box. Click it to open it when the result appears under Programs.

### CREATE A NEW CALENDAR

 5 minutes

If the calendar that opened doesn't have your name attached to it, simply follow these steps to create a new one just for you—or anyone else in your family who needs one:

1. In Windows Calendar, click File, and click New Calendar.

2. When the new calendar appears, type a name for it in the Calendars task pane on the left. Press Enter.

③ In the Details pane on the right, select the color you want to use.

If you can't see the Details pane, you can open it by clicking the View menu and clicking Details Pane.

That's it! Your calendar should look similar to the one shown in Figure 14-1. Now you're ready to move on to creating appointments and tasks.

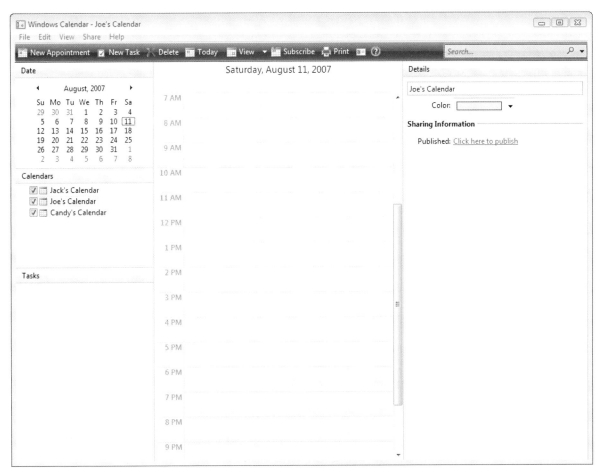

**Figure 14-1:** Windows Calendar is a simple-to-use calendar that you can use to coordinate not just your activities but those of everyone in the family.

## CREATE AN APPOINTMENT

**1 minute**

To create an appointment, follow these steps:

1. Click New Appointment on the toolbar. The appointment will appear on your calendar in the color you've chosen.

2. Type the details of the appointment in the Details pane on the right:

   - Type the title or details of the appointment in the New Appointment box.

   - Type any location information in the Location box.

   - Confirm you are in the correct calendar. Use the drop-down arrow in the Calendar box to select a new calendar for the appointment if necessary.

   - Under Appointment Information, type the date, time, recurring information, and whether this is an all-day appointment.

   - Select any reminder timing by using the drop-down arrow in the Reminder section.

   - Add participants.

   - Add notes.

3. Click the calendar itself to close the Details pane.

> **NOTE** When you have several calendars for your family, you can easily see appointments and tasks side by side by selecting the calendars you want to see in the task pane on the left, as shown in Figure 14-2. Simply click the calendars you want to see, and watch as the appointments and tasks appear on your calendar in the different colors family members have chosen. To see only certain calendars, deselect the other calendars.

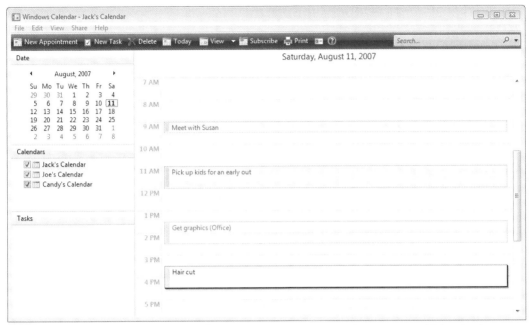

**Figure 14-2:** Selecting or deselecting calendars in the Calendars task pane lets you see multiple calendars at once so you can compare appointments and tasks.

## CREATE A TASK

**1 minute**

To create a task, follow these steps:

1. Click New Task on the toolbar.

2. In the New Task box in the Details pane, type a description for the task.

3. Click the calendar where you want the task to appear and add any related URLs.

4. Under Task Information, type the completion status, priority, and start and due dates.

5. Under Reminder, use the drop-down menu to select reminders.

6. Type any notes you want to add, and click the calendar to close the Details pane.

## SUBSCRIBE TO A CALENDAR ON THE WEB

 1 minute, not including the search time for the calendar you want

All kinds of organizations are placing their calendars on the Internet now. If they use the iCalendar format (.ics), you can subscribe to them and set how often your personal calendar is updated with new events. When you find a calendar you want to subscribe to, follow these steps:

1. Open Windows Calendar, and click Subscribe on the toolbar.

2. Type the URL of the calendar you found, and click Next.

3. Select a name for the calendar, an update interval, and whether you want reminders and tasks included.

4. Click Finish.

# Let the Windows Sidebar Be Your Second Set of Eyes

 5 minutes

You learned about the Windows Sidebar way back in Chapter 1, but we want to take a minute to show you how you can use it to keep you informed at all times. It's not just easy to do—it's fun. Dozens of gadgets exist that you can use, and more are being created daily. On the sample Windows Sidebar shown in Figure 14-3, we have a clock, a calendar, a search bar, a news feed, the weather, and a notepad. Kids can leave notes on the notepad for Mom, we can see the time clearly from the desktop, and we know at a glance whether the weather is nice enough to kick the kids outdoors. In addition, we know all the latest news and what's happening in the world around us.

That's what we mean by staying informed—use the Sidebar to give you the information you need at a glance. If you need to add gadgets to meet your needs, right-click the Sidebar, and click Add Gadgets. A gadget dialog box will display showing all the gadgets

**Figure 14-3:**
The Windows Sidebar can keep you informed with a glance.

you have on your system. Need more? Click Get More Gadgets Online to be taken directly to the Windows Vista Gadgets Gallery. Browse the categories, select the gadget you want, and download it. When it installs, it will automatically appear in your Sidebar as well as in your desktop gadget folder. Just drag and drop it to the Sidebar location you prefer.

As you select gadgets in the Windows Vista Gadgets Gallery, you'll see that some are available for your computer, some are for your Live.com site, and some are for your Windows Live Spaces space. Live.com and Windows Live Spaces are not part of Windows Vista; rather, they are Internet tools available from Microsoft. Look for gadgets that say "download"—those will download directly to your computer for use on the Sidebar.

Another point to consider as you download gadgets is that some are created by Microsoft, and some are freeware created by third parties. The Gadgets Gallery offers them all to you but will warn you when you attempt to download a gadget not certified by Microsoft. It doesn't mean those gadgets are malicious—but they could be. Just exercise caution when you download any of them!

# Play Games by Using Windows Vista and Media Center

 **5 minutes**

Bored? Tired of working and just need a break? We won't tell if you decide to play a game or two. Windows Vista comes installed with a few games for you, and you can always install new ones. These are the installed games shown in Figure 14-4:

- Solitaire
- FreeCell
- Minesweeper
- Spider Solitaire
- Hearts

- Chess Titans (*new*)
- Mahjong Titans (*new*)
- Purble Place (*new*)
- Inkball (*new*)

To find the games installed on your computer, you just need to open the Games folder. Click Start, and type **Games** in the Start Search box. When Games Explorer appears under Programs, click it. If you need instructions for playing a particular game, use Windows Help and Support.

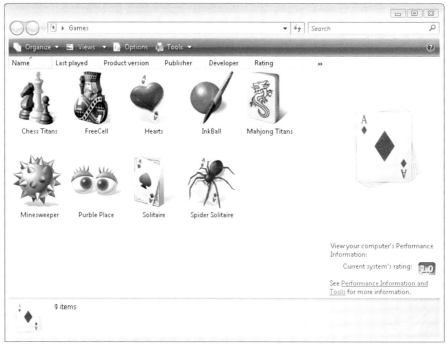

**Figure 14-4:** Eight games are automatically installed with Windows Vista. This example shows an extra game—Inkball—installed as well.

> **NOTE** You can open and play games from Windows Media Center, too. Go to the Start screen, scroll to Online Media, and then click Program Library. Just click the game you want to play.

# Protect Your Child with Parental Controls

We just talked about the different games you can play on Windows Vista and Windows Vista–based programs. The games provided by Microsoft with Windows Vista are all safe for your kids. But you might run into a problem here: Downloading games from the Internet can mean inappropriate games can be installed on your computer. Also, you may have other items on your computer that just aren't suitable for children. What's a parent to do? Take charge, and protect your kids from games and the like that may be too graphic or violent for them.

Windows Vista provides the Parental Controls feature to help you do this. You can set limits on how long your children can access the Internet, the hours they can spend on the computer in general, and which games they can play or programs they can run. When a program or Web site is blocked, a notification displays. Your child can click the link to request permission for access, but access is granted only when your account information is entered. (Hint: Keep your account information secret!) You can even generate activity reports to see what your child has been doing, so you'll never feel out of the loop again.

## TURN ON PARENTAL CONTROLS FOR A STANDARD USER

**10 minutes**

To turn on Parental Controls for a standard user, follow these steps:

1. Open Parental Controls through the Start Search box on the Start menu.

2. Select the user account to which to apply Parental Controls. The User Controls dialog box appears, as shown in Figure 14-5.

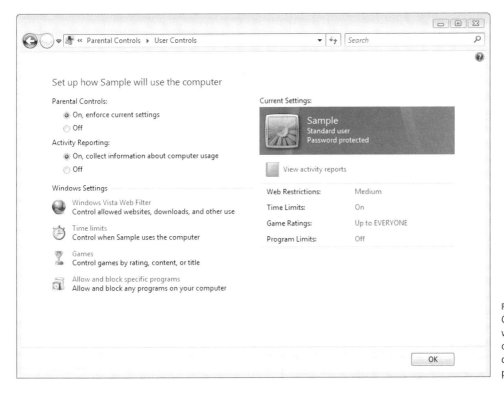

**Figure 14-5:** Parental Controls are an easy way to keep track of what your child is doing on the computer and the Internet.

③ Under Parental Controls, select On.

④ Under Activity Reporting, select On, Collect Information About Computer Usage.

⑤ Adjust the individual settings under Windows Settings:

**Windows Vista Web Filter**   Click this to decide which Web sites and content you want to allow or block, choose a Web restriction level, and block file downloads if you want to restrict the files your child downloads. Then click OK.

**Time Limits**   Click this to select the hours you want to allow computer usage and the hours you do not want your child using the computer. Then click OK.

**Games**   Click this to decide whether your child can play games at all. If yes, set the game ratings, and decide whether to block any specific games. Then click OK.

**Allow And Block Specific Programs**   Click this to decide whether your child can use all the programs on your computer or whether you want to restrict use to certain programs. If you restrict use, you need to select the programs that your child can use. Then click OK.

⑥ Click OK.

# Protect Your Investment with Windows Defender

Some software resides on your computer you might not be aware of. Don't panic—it's a good thing. It's called Windows Defender, and it protects you from malicious and unwanted software, such as viruses, spyware, and worms. These programs can try to install themselves on your computer anytime you connect to the Internet. They perform tasks on your computer without your consent such as popping up with advertising or collecting personal information about you. Scary, isn't it? Well, that's why Windows Vista comes with Windows Defender—to give you a good defense against nefarious types who want to hijack your computer.

One way to prevent spyware and other unwanted software from infiltrating your system (sounds like you're James Bond, doesn't it?) is to turn on real-time protection.

This will alert you instantly when a program is trying to install itself or run on your computer. As part of this protection, you can tell Windows Defender to display your computer's security status on the Quick Launch toolbar so you always know what your computer's status is.

## TURN ON WINDOWS DEFENDER REAL-TIME PROTECTION

**5 minutes**

To turn on Windows Defender real-time protection, follow these steps:

1. Go to Start, and type **Windows Defender** in the Start Search box. Click it to open when it appears under Programs.

2. Click Tools.

3. Click Options.

4. Select Use Real-Time Protection (Recommended) under Real-Time Protection Options:

   - Select the security options you want. (We suggest you select them all, but hey, maybe we're the only ones who like full protection.)

   - Make selections under Choose If Windows Defender Should Notify You About.

   - Select when you want the Windows Defender icon to appear as a notification.

5. Click Save.

You also can run periodic scans to be sure no unwanted or harmful software is lurking on your system. You can also see any actions that Defender has taken to prevent items from running on your computer without your consent (see Figure 14-6). To perform these tasks, Defender uses definitions to determine the threat level of software it detects on your computer. These definitions are kept up-to-date through integration with Windows Update, which automatically installs new definitions as they are released from Microsoft. As a result, you need to do two schedules: one to keep the Defender definitions up-to-date and one that schedules Defender to scan your computer for malicious programs.

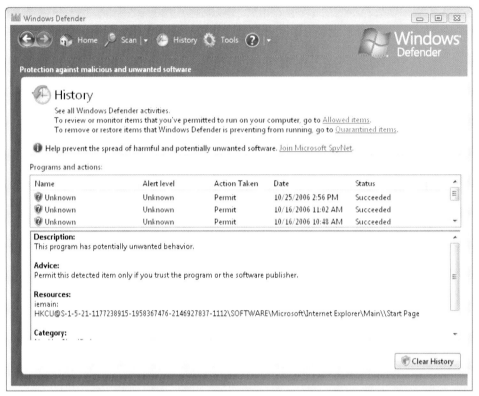

**Figure 14-6:** With Windows Defender, you can easily see everything that has been done to protect your computer.

## PUT WINDOWS DEFENDER DEFINITIONS ON A SCHEDULE

 **2 minutes**

To set a schedule to keep Windows Defender definitions up-to-date and to scan your computer for malicious and unwanted software, follow these steps:

1. Go to Start, and type **Windows Defender** in the Start Search box. Click it to open when it appears under Programs.

2. Click Tools.

3. Click Options.

④ Under Automatic Scanning, select Automatically Scan My Computer (Recommended):

- Using the drop-down menus, select a frequency, approximate time, and type of scan.

- Look for updated definitions before scanning.

- Select Apply Default Actions To Items Detected During A Scan to auto-matically remove unwanted spyware or other programs after a scan.

⑤ Under Default Actions, make changes using the drop-down menu if you do not want to use Windows Vista default alerts.

⑥ Click Save.

## A WORD ABOUT WINDOWS FIREWALL

Firewalls help prevent others from gaining access to your computer, and they help stop your computer from sending malicious software (unknown to you, of course) to other computers. Windows Vista comes with the Windows Firewall set to On. You can turn it off, but do that only if you have another firewall installed or you really like making yourself vulnerable to hackers, spyware, viruses, worms, and other nefarious programs. The On setting blocks a program from coming through unless you decide to unblock it by placing it on your exceptions list.

A third setting option is Block All Incoming Connections. This blocks all unsolicited attempts to connect to your computer. It's great if you're in a public WiFi zone, for example—you never know what's looking for you when you're off your own net-work connection. But be careful when choosing this option: This setting does not notify you when Windows Firewall is blocking a program, and it ignores any pro-grams on your exceptions list. You can still view most Web sites, receive e-mail, and use instant messaging, though.

## TURN ON WINDOWS FIREWALL

1 minute

To turn on Windows Firewall, follow these steps:

① Turn on Windows Firewall by going through the Control Panel or by using the Start Search box on the Start menu.

2. In the task pane on the left, click Turn Windows Firewall On Or Off. (Network policy settings may require an administrator password or confirmation.)

3. In the General tab, click On (Recommended).

4. Click OK.

> **NOTE** To permit exceptions, click the Exceptions tab, and select the items for which you want to allow an exception. Click OK when done.

# **Control** Windows Vista **with Your Voice**

 **1 hour**

We've already told you the basics about Windows Speech Recognition and how it works with Windows Media Center (see Chapter 12), but we wanted to add a few more points here because you can use it to control your computer—you can run programs besides Media Center, and you can even command Windows. You can also use it to dictate and edit text. For example, you can dictate into WordPad or fill out online forms in Windows Internet Explorer. You can use Windows Speech Recognition in so many ways that you owe it to yourself to try it.

We recommend you read Chapter 12 (although we can't imagine why you haven't already) to get a general understanding of how it works; then, take the Windows Speech Recognition tutorial to learn how to talk to your computer and learn how to train your computer to recognize your speech. Windows Help and Support has lists of dozens of commands that Windows Vista understands, so we won't list them here. But you have to try this! Who wants to be tied to a desk when they can be chasing a dog and multitasking on the computer at the same time?

> **NOTE** Windows Speech Recognition is not available in all languages. Select Speech Recognition Options to see the lists of available languages.

# GET AND USE WINDOWS LIVE MESSENGER

**5 minutes**

Come on, if you don't have Windows Live Messenger by now, you are *so* stuck in the '90s. This is a free instant messaging program that lets you chat with friends, share pictures and files with them, and make video or audio calls to them—in real time. Why use the phone when you can just that instantly appear on a friend's desktop?

If you didn't take the time to download Live Messenger when you read Chapter 1, do it now. To get it, go to the Start menu, and type **Messenger** in the Start Search box. Click Windows Live Messenger Download when it appears under Programs in the search results. This will take you to the Microsoft download page for the latest version of Live Messenger. Follow the instructions to download and install it. Then, once you have it installed, take a few minutes to set it up.

You can add anyone to your contacts list; they just have to be on Live Messenger as well. To find friends, type a name or e-mail address in the Find A Contact Or Number box, and press Enter. If a contact matches, the name will appear in the window. Messenger will prompt you to send an invitation to the contact, and once the two of you have connected, you can start communicating immediately and in real-time. Both of you must be online at the same time (duh!), but Live Messenger makes it easy to tell when your friends are available through the use of icons that display their status (I'm Busy, I'm Away, and so on). So stop reading this, and start yakking!

We hope you've had fun spicing up your life with Windows Calendar and the Windows Sidebar, not to mention all those games you can play. You learned a bit about how to protect yourself and your family with Windows Defender, and we hope you took the time for the speech recognition tutorial and training—that's going to be useful if you don't want to be tied down to your computer. You also learned about Windows Live Messenger and how it can help you stay in touch with family and friends.

- **Edit clip art in Word**

- **Create monthly calendars in Microsoft Office PowerPoint 2007**

- **Download and use Microsoft templates for personal items**

- **Plan your schedule with Microsoft Office Excel 2007**

- **Create your own coloring book**

- **Create your own greeting cards**

# **Incorporate** the 2007 Microsoft Office System

# CHAPTER 15

So, you have the Windows Vista operating system; you've learned how to do all the fun stuff with photos, videos, music, and television; and you have even started spicing up your life a bit with some of the cool features Windows Vista offers. It's time, then, to peek at the 2007 Microsoft Office system to see what kinds of fun things you can do with a combination of Windows Vista and the products that are part of the Microsoft Office system. Like us, you probably never imagined you could do the kinds of activities we'll talk about in this chapter. But that's the beauty of Windows Vista: It opens up a world you never knew existed.

*Windows Vista and the Microsoft Office system work great together, and you'll find that one without the other is sort of like cake with no icing... good, but so much better with the icing.*

The Microsoft Office system uses an interface that makes it quick and easy to find the commands and tools you need. A tabbed format lets you find general types of tools; groups on a tab help you find specific commands for the task you're handling. With these changes also come some intuitive aspects—if you insert clip art into a Microsoft Office Word 2007 document, for example, a Design tab will appear with a variety of design options for you. Click elsewhere in your Word 2007 document, and the Design tab disappears—you don't need it while you're working with text, for example, so it removes itself from your view. Click the clip art again, and it will reappear.

Since you have installed Windows Vista, we'll assume you have also upgraded or purchased the Microsoft Office system. That's smart. Windows Vista and the Microsoft Office system work great together, and you'll find that one without the other is sort of like cake with no icing...good, but so much better with the icing.

# Edit Clip Art in Office Word 2007

You know the feeling—you just want to use a cute little cartoon as embellishment for a note or a flyer, but it's too big or the wrong angle or a weird color. Word 2007 makes it easy to work with annoyances such as these. All you have to do is insert the clip art you want in the Word 2007 document you're working with and then double-click the art you want to change.

Doing this opens a Format tab at the top of your Word 2007 document. Suddenly, you have dozens of editing options! What shall you do? Let's start with the picture style first. This is a style set already created for you by Microsoft—a single click can take your clip art from a simple picture of a cat, for example, to a framed picture with a shadow behind it, as shown in Figure 15-1.

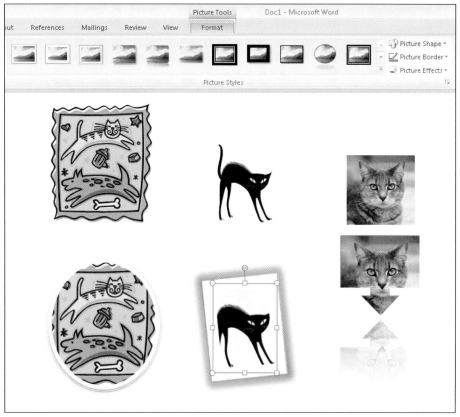

**Figure 15-1:** You can edit art in Word 2007 with just a few clicks—the art on the top is the original version, and the art on the bottom is the edited version.

## CHANGE THE STYLE OF YOUR ART

**2 minutes**

To instantly change the overall visual style of your art, follow these steps:

1. Double-click the art item you want to change.

2. On the Format tab, click the down arrow in the Picture Styles group. This will open the Picture Styles Quick Styles gallery.

3. Click the style you want to use for your art.

Okay, now that you have the style you want, you can play with picture shapes instead. This part is extra fun because it lets you take clip art and turn it into all kinds of shapes, such as an arrow, a banner, a star, or even a mathematic equation.

## CHANGE THE SHAPE OF YOUR ART

 2 minutes

To change the shape of your art, follow these steps:

1 Double-click the art item you want to change.

2 On the Format tab, click Picture Shape in the Picture Styles group. This will open the Picture Shape Quick Styles gallery.

3 Click the shape you want to use for your art.

Not enough pizzazz for you yet? Add a border or an effect—those are equally easy to do.

## ADD A BORDER TO YOUR ART

 2 minutes

To add a border to your art, follow these steps:

1 Double-click the art item to which you want to add a border.

2 On the Format tab, click Picture Border in the Picture Styles group. This will open the Picture Border Quick Styles gallery where you can choose from themes or standard colors, add weight to your border, and turn your border into a dashed line.

3 Click the option you want to use for your border.

The final way you can edit your clip art easily in Word 2007 is through the Picture Effects command. This adds visual effects, such as glows, shadows, reflections, and three-dimensional (3-D) effects.

## ADD A VISUAL EFFECT TO YOUR ART

 **2 minutes**

To add a visual effect to your art, follow these steps:

1. Double-click the art item to which you want to add a border.

2. On the Format tab, click Picture Effects in the Picture Styles group. This will open the Picture Effects Quick Styles gallery where you can choose from preset effects or create your own shadow, reflection, glow, soft edge, bevel, or 3-D rotation.

3. Click the option you want to use for your border.

# Create Monthly Calendars in Office PowerPoint 2007

Okay, so you don't want to use Windows Calendar because you're just not that in to tracking your life on the computer. You prefer a pen, pencil, crayon, or some other handheld medium to mark down appointments, and you want to add your own photos or art to the calendar to personalize it. Maybe calendar art on your refrigerator or wall is the closest you will ever get to displaying Picasso in your home. Fine. Open Microsoft Office PowerPoint 2007, and create your own calendar already, won't you?

 **5 to 30 minutes, depending on your creativity**

To create a monthly calendar in PowerPoint 2007, follow these steps:

1. Open a new document in PowerPoint 2007.

2. In Help, type the year, and type **Calendar**. For example, type **2008 Calendar**.

3. Choose the calendar template you want from the search results.

4. Click Download Now. The calendar will download into PowerPoint 2007. You can make it even prettier, as shown in Figure 15-2, with the following options:

    - To change the theme or design, select a new one on the Design tab in the Themes group.

- To change the font, click Fonts in the Themes group on the Design tab.

- To change the background, click Background Styles in the Background group on the Design tab.

> **TIP** You can add pictures to your calendar background by selecting Format Background under Background Styles. Click Fill, select Picture Or Texture Fill, and click File under Insert From. Locate the picture, click Insert, and then click Close.

⑤ To print, click the Microsoft Office Button, and click Print. Select the print options you prefer.

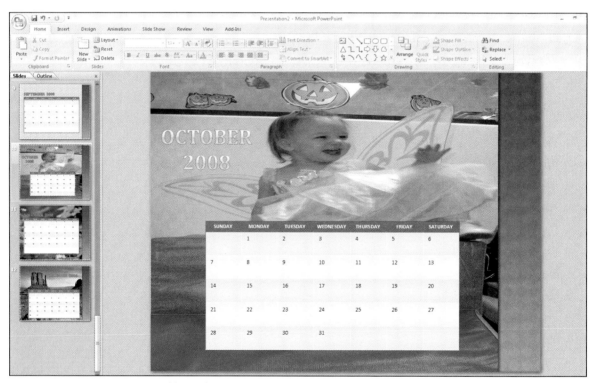

Figure 15-2: Get as creative as you like, and invent your own calendar in PowerPoint 2007.

# Download and Use Microsoft Templates

One Web site that should be on your list of Favorites is the Templates page at Microsoft Office Online. This place has almost anything you can think of, and if it doesn't, you can modify the templates it does provide to create something unique and personal of your own. If you're not familiar with templates, they are already-created documents that you can download and tweak to meet your needs. For example, if you want to create a family budget, you don't need to start from scratch—just download Family Monthly Budget for Excel, and fill in the blanks with your own information. Or maybe you want to create a resume but don't know how to format it. The Templates page has basic, job-specific and situation-specific resume formats for you to use. Insert your information, and start applying for jobs. It's truly that easy!

You can access the Microsoft Office Online templates through Help in any Office 2007 program you're using—type the kind of template you're seeking, and a list will appear of all the available templates that match your search term. Or go directly to *www.office.microsoft.com*. Click Templates, and then simply search for new templates or click Browse Templates to find something specific.

Here are some examples of the kinds of personal templates available from Microsoft:

- Credit card use log

- Diet and exercise charts (nutrition journal, weight-loss tracker, fitness charts, food fat percentage calculator, daily logs)

- Home and auto care (contents inventory list, home maintenance schedule, vehicle service record)

- Planners and schedulers (personal and family budgets, meal planner, wedding planner, homework planner, residential move planner, party planner, and more)

- Signs (garage sale, fundraisers, car for sale, parties, miscellaneous)

- Travel and maps (travel itinerary, travel check list for plane, travel plan, expense reports, booking forms, maps of continents)

- Genealogy maps (requests for genealogy records, family history book)

If you have a Windows Live ID, you can even store templates directly online for access from any computer with an Internet connection. You can submit your own templates too if you come up with one that isn't already available.

We'll now cover a few of the tasks you can perform with templates.

# Plan Your Schedule with Office Excel 2007

Calendars are great, but sometimes it's nice to just have a schedule in your pocket or one to post for the babysitter. Microsoft Office Excel 2007 has some templates that make creating a printed schedule super simple to do—just download the template, fill in some blanks, and then head out the door. By the way, these are also great for planning meetings—you can impress the boss with your uber-organizational skills by tossing one of these on her desk.

**5 minutes**

To create a schedule with Excel, follow these steps:

    **1**  Open a new document in Excel 2007.

    **2**  In Help, type **schedule**, as shown in Figure 15-3.

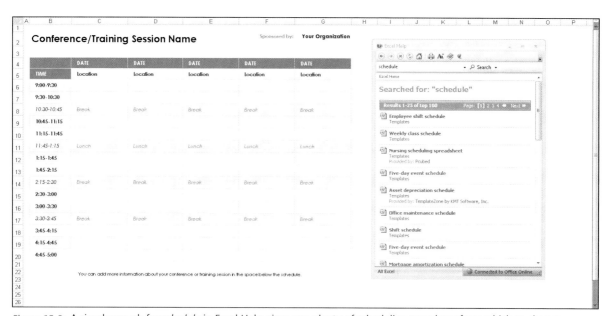

Figure 15-3: A simple search for *schedule* in Excel Help gives you plenty of scheduling templates from which to choose.

③ Select the schedule you prefer. Click Download Now.

④ Fill in the blanks with your information.

⑤ Print or save the document by using the Microsoft Office Button Print or Save selections.

# Create Your Own Coloring Book

If you have kids, your home harbors more coloring books than a rabbit has babies. Chances are, those books are half-used because your kids got bored with the pictures and concepts. If that's the case, you need to create coloring books that are tailored to your child's interests. We'll show you how to take a template and turn it into a coloring book to meet any child's fantasy.

**10 to 30 minutes, depending on your creativity**

To create your own coloring book, follow these steps:

① Go to Microsoft Office Online at *www.office.microsoft.com*.

② Click Templates.

③ Type **coloring book** in the search box. Select Dinosaur Coloring Book from the search results, and download it. This will open a Word 2007 document, as shown in Figure 15-4.

④ Print the book, and staple it together if your child likes dinosaurs. If your child is interested in something else, click Dinosaur, and select Edit Text in the Text group on the Format tab. Change the text to the new topic, and go to step 5.

⑤ To change clip art, select the art you want to change, and click Delete.

⑥ Click Clip Art in the Illustrations group on the Insert tab. In the search box, type the new terms, and click Go.

⑦ Select the new piece of art, and resize it to the size you want for the page.

⑧ Follow these instructions for editing clip art in Word 2007 to turn each piece of clip art into a simple black outline—just delete the colors you don't want, and replace them with black borders, as shown in Figure 15-5.

⑨ Print the coloring book, and staple the pages together.

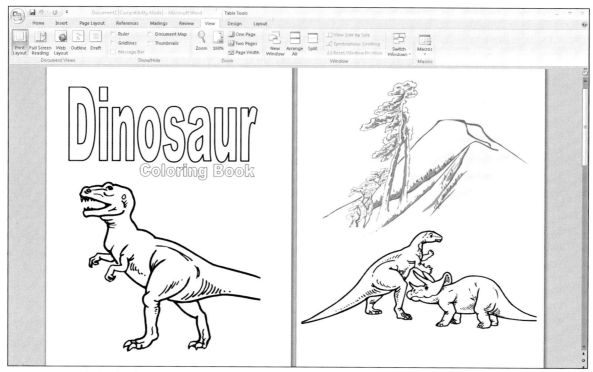

**Figure 15-4:** A coloring book template from Microsoft Office Online that you can modify to delight any child.

**Figure 15-5:** You can easily edit colored clip art to create simple black-and-white drawings for your coloring book.

**TIP** Right-click clip art to edit it quickly. For example, if the clip art you chose has a green circle attached to it, you can remove it by right-clicking the art and selecting Edit Picture. Click the green circle, and delete it.

# Create Your Own Greeting Cards with Office Publisher 2007

If you're like us, you're tired of spending ridiculous amounts of money on 20 greeting cards that don't really say what you want them to say in the first place. Yes, we're cheap. But we also like to personalize the cards we do send to friends and family, and there's no better way to do it than by using Microsoft Office Publisher 2007. Yes, we said it: Print your own cards, and use the money you'll save to buy fancy labels for your envelopes. Or buy a Ferrari. We don't care; just don't spend it on tacky cards that anyone else can buy. This probably won't take you the 15 minutes stated, but we are allotting you that much time so you can sift through all the designs and layouts.

 **15 minutes**

To create your own greeting cards, follow these steps:

1. Open Microsoft Office Publisher 2007.

2. Under Publication Types, select Greeting Cards.

3. Click a design provided or download a design from Microsoft Office Online. For our purposes, we'll assume you chose a design provided.

4. Under Customize (in the task pane on the right), select the color and font schemes.

5. Under Options, select a page size and layout. Notice that under Layout, you are given dozens more options depending on the selection you make.

6. At the bottom right of your screen, click Create.

Your card will appear with four pages available for personalization. The page numbers appear at the bottom of your screen. Click each page, and make the text changes you want in the card itself. Don't forget page 4—you can add your own name as the creator of the card so recipients know you really did create the card yourself. You can change or add pictures to your cards, play with designs, and get creative with the text. It's your design, so do whatever you want (see Figure 15-6)!

**Figure 15-6:** Here is a sample of a greeting card you can create in Publisher 2007.

In the Format Publication pane, you have another chance to change fonts, colors, templates, and even the page size. When you're satisfied, print the card, and find an envelope and stamp. Don't forget to sign and mail it!

In this chapter, we gave you a quick glimpse into how the Microsoft Office 2007 system can complement Windows Vista with cool creations such as coloring books, greeting cards, personalized calendars, and schedules. Get creative, and don't be afraid to play with the Microsoft Office 2007 system—you're going to find many more items that you can use in your daily life.

- Navigate the interface

- Navigate quickly using the Quick Tabs feature

- Set up tab groups

- Take advantage of the Search box

- Print Web pages so they look like Web pages

- Configure RSS feeds

- Double-check security

- Use Windows CardSpace to manage your passwords

# **Surf** with Windows Internet Explorer 7

# CHAPTER 16

The Internet is a pretty simple concept, really. Type the URL for the site you want to visit, and start reading. But sometimes you see something on the Web page that makes you click a link to find out more. A new window pops up. Then you click another link to produce yet another window. Before you know it, you're smothered in windows and can't figure out where you started. That—and more—has all changed with Windows Internet Explorer 7 in Windows Vista. The simple interface, the tabbed browsing system, and the improved search and security features of Internet Explorer 7 will impress you, we promise.

Internet Explorer 7 uses some of the same features that make both the Windows Vista operating system and the 2007 Microsoft Office system so easy to use. It offers additional cool features too, such as the ability to print Web pages in full without losing content and the ability to use add-ons that save you time such as autofill forms.

In this chapter, we'll explore the highlights of Internet Explorer 7 instead of covering every single feature it offers. Let's get started!

# Navigate the Interface

**20 minutes**

You'll see some familiar features in Internet Explorer 7, such as the Back and Forward buttons (now arrows) and the Address bar. But you'll probably first notice the tabbed interface that lets you open multiple Web pages by using just one window—each new page is accessed via the tabs you see, as shown in Figure 16-1. In this figure, at the top of the screen—just below the Address bar—is a large tab showing MSN.com. There are two other active tabs and a smaller tab. These tabs are the heart of Internet Explorer 7. Go ahead and click the smaller tab. A message appears telling you that you've opened a new tab. This is called *tabbed browsing*: Each new tab is a new Web page, but it opens in the single Web browser you initially opened. Clicking a different tab in the browser takes you to a different Web site—without opening a new window. It's cool, and once you use this, you will never want to return to the multiple-window browser concept again.

*The simple interface, the tabbed browsing system, and the improved search and security features of Internet Explorer 7 will impress you, we promise.*

Another new aspect to the interface is the Live Search box in the upper-right corner of the window. Click the down arrow, and you'll see the default is Live Search, a Microsoft search function. Type the word **dog** in the Live Search box, and press Enter. Now the Web page has shifted instantly to the search results for the word *dog*—cool, huh? You didn't have to go to a separate Web page to conduct an Internet search; you just typed the word in your browser, and bam! Results appear. We'll show you how to change the search defaults later in this chapter.

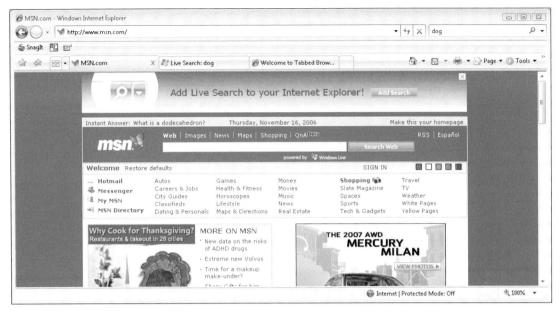

**Figure 16-1:** Internet Explorer 7 uses a tabbed format to make surfing the Web simple and fast.

Look immediately to the left of the tabs in your window. Do you see the tiny button with four squares? Click it. You've just opened Quick Tabs—a feature that lets you see all the tabs in your window at once. It gives you a thumbnail view of up to 20 open tabs at once.

> **NOTE** You must have more than one tab in use before you can see the Quick Tabs option.

Immediately to the left of the Quick Tabs button is a button with a yellow star and a green plus sign. This is the Add To Favorites button. Click it, and you'll see the familiar Add To Favorites command. Below that, however, is a new command: Add Tab Group To Favorites. This command lets you organize multiple tabs into a single group and then save that group as a Favorite. Let's say you have saved all your dog Web sites into a Dog tab group in your Favorites menu. In the new Favorites Center (the button with the single large star), a single click will open all the sites in the tab group. The Favorites Center will expand as you add more sites to Internet Explorer 7; this is where

Really Simple Syndication (RSS) feeds, Favorites, and browsing history reside. One final area of the interface to review is the toolbar, located directly below the Live Search box. This is where you will find Print, Save, Page Setup, and other familiar commands. Look closely, and you'll also see a new button that lets you view all RSS feeds on the open page (we'll talk more about that later, too!).

NOTE **Add-ons for Internet Explorer are available at** *www.ieaddons.com.* **These are items that help personalize the way you use the Internet, and they can make it easier and faster to get the information you need. Parental controls, animation, privacy, and other add-ons are available. Microsoft is always updating the add-ons it provides, so return often for the latest offering.**

# ARE YOU PHISHING BAIT?

As you conducted your first search, the Microsoft Phishing Filter dialog box may have appeared. Phishing occurs when an e-mail is sent falsely claiming to be from an established, legitimate enterprise. It usually entices you to visit a Web site, where you are asked for personal information. The problem is that this Web site is bogus—it's a copy of the true site, and the personal information you give the site will be used for fraudulent purposes. The sender is sending this bait to thousands, hoping a few fish will bite. Hence, it's called *phishing*.

We strongly suggest you select Turn On Automatic Phishing Filter (Recommended) in the dialog box, and click OK. This selection means Internet Explorer 7 will warn you (as shown in the graphic on the next page) when you attempt to visit a potentially untrustworthy site with colored warnings in a security status bar at the top of your Internet Explorer 7 window. Yellow means the site might have potential problems; red is a confirmed phishing destination—you will automatically be navigated away from the site. If you didn't see a Microsoft Phishing Filter dialog box but want to be sure your phishing filter is turned on, click Tools on the Internet Explorer 7 toolbar. Click Phishing Filter, and verify you see the Turn Off Automatic Web Site Checking command. If you do, your filter is turned on. If not, you will see Turn On Automatic Web Site Checking. Click that option, and you're all set.

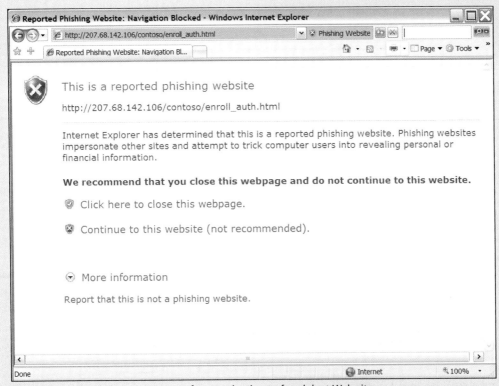

The phishing filter helps prevents you from navigating to fraudulent Web sites.

## **Use** Quick **Tabs**

 **2 minutes**

We mentioned the Quick Tabs feature earlier. Here's the deal: Even though the tabbed browsing concept is so cool, it *is* possible to have so many tabs open that you lose track of which tab houses which Web page. Maybe you're someone who likes to open 20 pages at once and bounce between them; that's fine. (It's a little excessive perhaps, but it's fine by us.) If you lose track of which tab holds which Web page, click the Quick Tabs button we mentioned earlier. Every Web page you have opened will appear in a thumbnail format, as shown in Figure 16-2, so you can look for the Web page you want. When you find it, click the thumbnail, and you'll be taken automatically to the tab with that Web page.

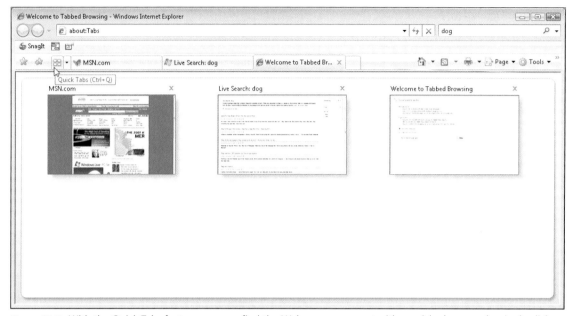

**Figure 16-2:** With the Quick Tabs feature, you can find the Web page you want with a quick glance and a single click.

# Set Up Tab Groups

**5 minutes**

Let's talk about tab groups a bit more. If you're like us, you don't stop at just one Web site when you're researching a subject. Instead, you dig up all the sites you can find, read through them all, and then save the individual pages you like as Favorites. You might even be super organized and create folders inside your Favorites so you can easily find those sites again. When you need them, you go to your Favorites and open each one separately.

With tab groups, you can vastly reduce all that grouping and searching and opening. In your browser, open three sites on any topic you like. We chose three sites from our search on dogs. Close any other windows that don't relate to the topic you've chosen so all you have are three tabs open to Web pages about your topic. Now you're ready to set up a tab group.

## CREATE A TAB GROUP

To create a tab group, follow these steps:

**1** In Internet Explorer 7, click the Add To Favorites button.

**2** Click Add Tab Group To Favorites.

**3** Type a name for the group in Tab Group Name.

**4** Select Favorites in Create In.

**5** Click Add.

## OPEN A TAB GROUP

To open a tab group, follow these steps:

**1** In Internet Explorer 7, click the Favorites button.

**2** Click the tab group you want to open.

**3** To the right of the tab group, you'll see a blue arrow. Click the arrow, as shown in Figure 16-3. All the pages in that tab group will open for you.

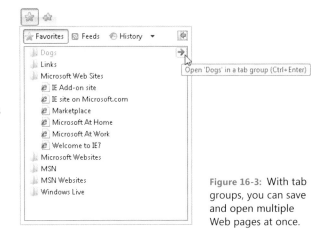

Figure 16-3: With tab groups, you can save and open multiple Web pages at once.

# Take Advantage of the Live Search Box

**5 minutes**

The Live Search feature in Internet Explorer 7 will save you so much time! We use this feature constantly because it lets you choose a search provider from a drop-down list of providers that you select. Live Search is the default search engine, but you can change that to Google, Yahoo, or whatever search engine you prefer. When one search engine doesn't return the results you were seeking, just select another provider from the drop-down list. Internet Explorer 7 remembers the search term and transfers it to the new search engine. Use this once, and you'll have the hang of it.

## ADD MORE PROVIDERS TO LIVE SEARCH

To add more providers to Live Search, follow these steps:

1. In Internet Explorer 7, click the down arrow next to the Live Search box.

2. Click Find More Providers. A list will appear of both Web and topic search providers.

3. Click the search provider you want. You can add other search providers not shown by following the instructions in the Create Your Own section of the page.

4. Click Add Provider in the dialog box that appears, as shown in Figure 16-4. If you want a particular search provider to become the new default, select the Make This My Default Search Provider box.

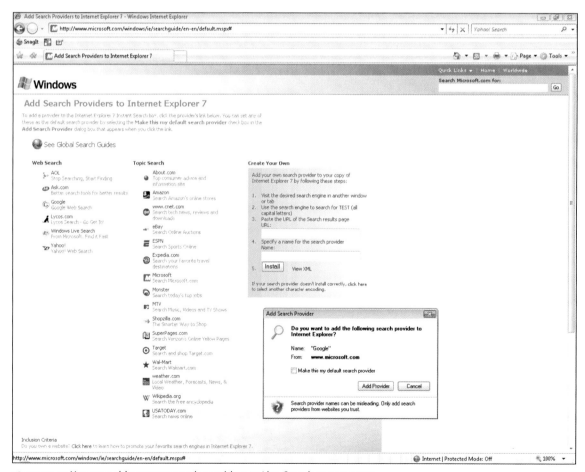

**Figure 16-4:** You can add as many search providers to Live Search as you want.

# Use Advanced Printing Features

 5 minutes

When was the last time you tried to print a Web page? The chances are good you don't try it often! Printouts rarely seem to contain all the information shown on the page; the side of the page might be missing, or the content comes out looking really weird. That problem has been eliminated with Internet Explorer 7.

An Internet Explorer 7 default setting shrinks a Web page's text just enough to ensure the entire page prints properly, and Print Preview lets you adjust page margins, layout, headers, and footers and lets decrease or increase the print space as needed. What? Print a Web page that actually looks like the Web page you saw? What a concept.

## PREVIEW YOUR WEB PAGE BEFORE PRINTING

To preview your Web page before printing, follow these steps:

1. In Internet Explorer 7, click the Print button.

2. Click Print Preview.

3. Review the page on the screen:

   - To change the page orientation, use the Portrait and Landscape buttons.
   - To adjust the headers, footers, letter size, paper source, and margins, click Page Setup, and then make changes in the dialog box that appears. Click OK when finished.
   - To change the view, select from the Page View drop-down menu, or click the Full Width or Full Page button. You can see multiple pages at once by selecting a multipage view in the drop-down menu.
   - To change the Print Size, select the option you prefer from the drop-down menu.

# Configure RSS Feeds

RSS feeds provide updated content from a Web site. News, sports, weather, new products, whatever—when a site offers this kind of feed and you add it to your Favorites, you get the latest information about the topic every time you access the page. When Internet Explorer 7 senses an RSS feed, the Feeds button turns a lovely shade of red to get your attention. Click the button, and the Web page will switch to a page showing you the RSS feeds available.

## SUBSCRIBE TO A FEED

 **2 minutes**

To subscribe to a feed, follow these steps:

1. When Internet Explorer 7 shows you a feed is available, a Subscribe To This Feed link will appear, as shown in Figure 16-5. Click the link.

2. In the Subscribe To This Feed dialog box, decide whether to rename the feed or keep the name provided.

3. Click Subscribe. A message will appear on your screen telling you the subscription has been successful.

---

Yahoo! Search: dogs

**You are viewing a feed that contains frequently updated content.** When you subscribe to a feed, it is added to the Common Feed List. Updated information from the feed is automatically downloaded to your computer and can be viewed in Internet Explorer and other programs. Learn more about feeds.

⚜ Subscribe to this feed

---

Figure 16-5: You can subscribe to RSS feeds with a single click.

## CONFIGURE FEED PROPERTIES

 **4 minutes**

To configure feed properties, follow these steps:

1. Open the Favorites Center to access your feeds.

2. Click the feed you want to configure.

3. On the right side of your screen, click View Feed Properties.

4. Click Settings under Update Schedule in the Feed Properties box to update the feed schedule. You can specify how often feeds are downloaded, decide whether feeds should automatically be marked as read, decide whether they should play sounds, or turn on a feed reading view. Click OK when finished.

5. In the Feed Properties dialog box, set the maximum number of updates you want to save in the Archive section.

6. Click OK.

# **Verify** Security

Before you run off unsupervised on the Internet, take some time to verify your security options. We've discussed the phishing filter, but you should also review your pop-up blocker settings and look for updates for your computer. Remember, hackers, worms, viruses, and spyware don't care how nice you are; they want your information, and they want to use your computer to do bad things. Take the time to keep them off your system.

### VERIFY YOUR POP-UP BLOCKER SETTINGS

 5 minutes

To verify your pop-up blocker settings, follow these steps:

1. Click Tools on the toolbar.
2. Click Pop-Up Blocker:

   - Be sure it says Turn Off Pop-Up Blocker. This means the blocker is turned on; the only option is to turn it off.

   - Select Pop-Up Blocker Settings to allow pop-ups from specified Web sites. In the Notifications And Filter Level area, ensure both Play A Sound When A Pop-Up Is Blocked and Show Information Bar When A Pop-Up Is Blocked are selected. Your filter level should be at least Medium.

3. Click Close.

### CHECK YOUR PHISHING FILTER SETTINGS

 5 minutes

The phishing filter has numerous options. Unless you are an experienced computer user, we recommend you leave all the settings at the defaults set by Microsoft. However, everyone should verify that automatic Web site checking is turned on:

1. Click Tools on the toolbar.
2. Click Phishing Filter.

Be sure it says Turn Off Automatic Website Checking.

# WHAT IS **WINDOWS CARDSPACE?**

A cool feature in Windows Vista called Windows CardSpace helps you create relationships with Web sites and online services. In a nutshell, it stores a digital identity for you on a card that you complete and then give to Web sites as needed. Why, you might ask, would anyone want or need such a thing? Well, as you use the Internet, you're probably discovering that more and more sites require passwords and user IDs, which means you have to track all those accounts and passwords. After a while, you get "password fatigue"—you get tired of typing different information for every site, so you get a bit lazy and reuse the same account names, passwords, and IDs at multiple locations.

This fatigue can result in online identity theft, fraud, and privacy issues. That's where CardSpace comes in. It's a single identification system that lets you create and choose from a portfolio of identities called *information cards* and distribute them to different Web sites. You can use each card for certain situations, and the information on it is called *claims*. Claims can be your age, your address, your cat's name...anything that makes sense for a particular purpose. Just as your driver's license is authenticated by a state licensing system, your information card contains information that is authenticated by you, a Web site provider, or a third party.

Not every site will accept the same information card when it tries to identify you— you can't use your business card as a credit card in a store, for example—so you need a variety of cards in your portfolio to handle different situations. CardSpace helps you create the right cards for your needs. Once you have created your cards, you select which ones to send to Web sites and online services.

We could go on for pages explaining more about the concept, but we'll stop with that basic explanation. If you decide to use Windows CardSpace, follow the steps in the "Create a Windows CardSpace Card" section to get started.

## CREATE A WINDOWS CARDSPACE CARD

 **8 minutes**

To create a Windows CardSpace card, follow these steps:

1. Click the Start button, type **Windows CardSpace** in the Start Search box, and click to open it when it appears in the search results.

② In the Select A Card To Preview dialog box, click Add A Card under Your Cards. Click OK.

③ Click Create A Personal Card.

④ In the Edit A New Card dialog box, type a name for the card under Card Properties. You can also add a picture here if you like.

⑤ Choose the information you are comfortable sharing under Information that you can send with this card.

⑥ Click Save.

When a Web site requests a card, as shown in Figure 16-6, only the cards that contain the claims the site requires will be highlighted in your CardSpace collection. Just click a card that meets the requirements, and send it. We suggest you use the Help feature in CardSpace to learn more about when and where to use identification cards. Microsoft, by the way, never sees the data—unless you choose to send one of your cards to a Microsoft Web site.

**Log in to our Community**

Please log in to your account by either entering your username and password below or by selecting the Windows CardSpace Information Card that you have linked to your account.

Sign in with your username and password

Sign in name

Password                    (I forgot my password)
                ☑ Next time automatically sign me in
                Sign in »

OR

Sign in with your Information Card

**Information Card**

                Sign in »

Figure 16-6: As information cards become more common, you'll see more sites asking for your card in order to sign in.

Now you see why we like Internet Explorer 7 so much! If you spend any time at all online, you'll quickly appreciate how useful the tabbed interface is as well as how simple it is to search the Web. Toss in the advanced printing features, easy-to-configure RSS feeds, improved security, and CardSpace, and you have a Web browser that can really do battle for you.

- Use Windows Mail for safe communications

- Use Windows Contacts to stay organized

- Set your RSS options to stay informed

- Take advantage of network features for easy control

- Use the Remote Desktop Connection and Remote Assistance to work and get help from home

# **Make** the Most of Windows Vista Extras

# CHAPTER 17

In this chapter, we're going to cover a lot of ground. Networks, remote computers, mail—the tasks you do every day just might be a little easier if you know how to take advantage of some "extra" features and programs offered by the Windows Vista operating system. The first step, of course, is knowing these features and programs exist. The second step is using them to your advantage. We'll tell you where these features are; it's up to you how much or how little you let Windows Vista simplify your life.

# **Use** Windows Mail

 **30 minutes**

Got mail? Of course you do. Your electronic mailbox is probably crammed with hundreds or even thousands of e-mails that you are loathe to delete. We bet that at least half of those e-mails are junk mail and that you waste a good portion of time digging through all those e-mails to find the one that really needs a response. It's time, then, to get serious about your mail and get Windows Mail.

*Most people use networks in office settings, but they are becoming more common at home as Dad uses the laptop in the kitchen, Mom finishes some work in the basement, and the kids play games in the living room.*

Windows Mail is the successor to Outlook Express. It lets you manage three types of electronic accounts: mail, news (newsgroups), and directory services (online address books). The cool part is that it has three key features that will reduce the clutter and annoyance of the standard e-mail inbox:

**Instant search**   A built-in search box like the one you have been using in Windows Vista

**Junk mail filter**   A built-in filter that automatically screens e-mail (no "training" required) to identify and separate junk e-mail

**Phishing filter**   A filter that analyzes e-mails to detect fraudulent links

> **NOTE** *Instant search* works the same way as it does anywhere else in Windows Vista. Just type the topic or phrase you want to find, and press Enter.

## GET STARTED WITH WINDOWS MAIL

To use Windows Mail, you need to be sure you are connected to the Internet and have an e-mail address. Next, open Windows Mail by using the Start menu. The first time you start it, you will need to type your Internet service provider (ISP) connection information (the names of both your incoming e-mail server and your outgoing e-mail server, as well as any applicable passwords) and e-mail address, as shown in Figure 17-1. If you don't know what your connection information is, you can get it from your ISP.

Once that you have typed that information, you have added your e-mail account and are ready to start sending and receiving e-mail. Just like with any other e-mail program, you can create, forward, and reply to mail. Figure 17-2 gives you an example of a sample e-mail message. Windows Mail will look for new mail whenever it starts and every 30 minutes after that.

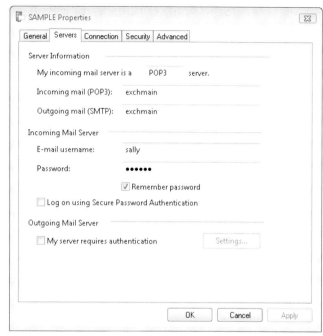

Figure 17-1: To create a Windows Mail account, you need basic information about your incoming and outgoing mail servers.

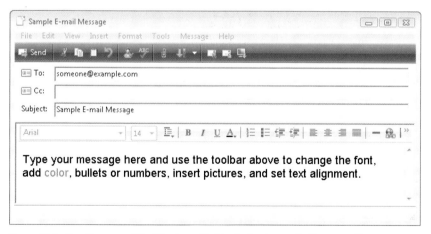

Figure 17-2: Creating e-mail in Windows Mail is similar to most other e-mail programs.

## IMPORT INFORMATION INTO WINDOWS MAIL

If you are upgrading your computer from a previous version of Windows, mail from Outlook Express will automatically be imported into Windows Mail. But if you use another e-mail program, you will need to take some steps to import messages on your own.

## IMPORT MESSAGES TO WINDOWS MAIL

To import messages to Windows Mail, follow these steps:

1. Open Windows Mail.

2. Click File, point to Import, and then click Messages.

3. In the Windows Import Mail dialog box, select the program from which you want to import your messages. Click Next.

4. Follow the instructions for your particular mail program.

> **NOTE** Windows Mail does not import account settings when it imports messages. You need to import those separately. Click the File menu, click Accounts, click Import, and then click Mail Account Settings. Follow the instructions provided.

## CREATE AND MANAGE FOLDERS

One way to keep yourself from going crazy with all the e-mails you receive is to file them in folders. It's a basic organizational method, and it really does make it easier to store and find messages when you need them. For example, you might create a folder called Pictures to store messages with attached photos or one called Work to separate business e-mails from personal e-mails.

## CREATE A FOLDER

**1 minute**

To create a folder, follow these steps:

1. Open Windows Mail.

2. Click File, and point to New.

3. Click Folder.

4. Type a name for the folder in the Folder Name box.

5. Select a location for the folder by clicking one in the Select The folder In Which To Create The New Folder list.

6. Click OK.

One way to manage your folders is to create a rule that automatically drops e-mails into the folders you have created. For example, when an e-mail arrives from a co-worker, you can designate that it automatically move to the Work folder you have created. You can also create rules to flag specific messages for action later or to delete messages so you never even see them. (This is handy for notes from an ex-wife/husband/boyfriend/girlfriend!)

## CREATE A RULE

**2 to 3 minutes**

To create a rule, follow these steps:

1. Open Windows Mail.

2. Click Tools, and point to Message Rules.

3. Click Mail.

4. Select the conditions for your rule. (For example, specify Where The From Line Contains People.)

5. Select the actions for your rule. (For example, specify Delete It.)

6. In Rule Description, click any underlined values to add more specific details. See Figure 17-3 for an example.

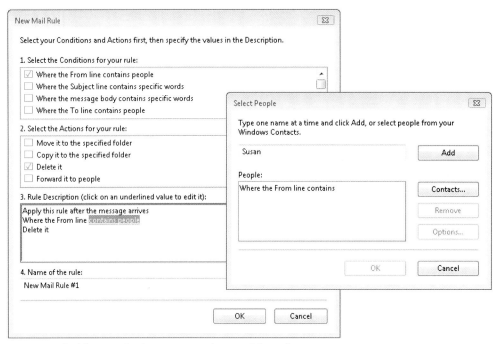

**Figure 17-3:** In this example, the user wanted any mail from Susan to automatically be deleted when it arrived.

**7** Click Add, and click OK.

**8** Look at the Rule Description box again to be sure the rule reads exactly the way you want it to read. Click OK, and then click OK in the Message Rules dialog box.

## CREATE CUSTOM STATIONERY

You can create your very own stationery in Windows Mail, and you can do it pretty quickly. You can choose from a variety of stationery designs, plus you can even save stationery that someone else sends you and steal it for your own use. (Go ahead, we won't tell!)

## CREATE YOUR OWN STATIONERY

5 minutes

To create your own stationery, follow these steps:

1. Open Windows Mail.

2. Click Tools.

3. Click Options.

4. Click Compose. Choose the font, stationery, and even business card information you want to include.

5. Click the Create New button to use the stationery wizard—it will help you create a background picture, choose colors, and more. Click Finish when you're done, and then click OK.

## USE YOUR STATIONERY

1 minute

To use your stationery, follow these steps:

1. Open Windows Mail.

2. Click Message, and select New Message Using. Click the name of the stationery you want to use.

3. Type your message in the New Message dialog box that appears.

## SAVE SOMEONE ELSE'S STATIONERY FOR YOUR OWN USE

1 minute

To save someone else's stationery for your own use, follow these steps:

1. Open the message.

2. Click the File menu, and click Save As Stationery.

# GO AHEAD—USE **THE NEWSGROUPS!**

It's easy to use Windows Mail to access Microsoft Help newsgroups. Just click Microsoft Communities in the folder pane. The first time you do this, you'll need to download newsgroups and turn on communities. It will take just a few minutes to download; then you just scroll through all the available newsgroups, subscribe to the ones you want, and click OK. After that, your list of newsgroups will appear under Microsoft Communities, and you can access individual newsgroups with a single click.

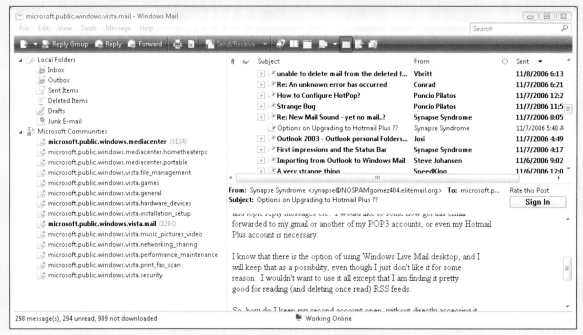

You can easily subscribe to and access newsgroups by using Windows Mail.

## **Add** Windows Contacts

Now that you know how to set up and use Windows Mail, you should learn a little bit about the Windows Contacts feature. *Contacts* store information about people and organizations so you can easily send e-mails to individuals or multiple people at once. Open Windows Contacts through the Start button (you know how we like to use that Search function!), and then perform the following steps to add or delete contacts. Depending how fast you type, you can add contacts in seconds. Seriously. Would we lie to you? Tease you, yes. Lie to you, never!

**2 minutes**

To add a contact, follow these steps:

1. In Windows Contacts, click New Contact.

2. In the Contact Properties dialog box, type any information applicable to the contact by using the tabs across the top, as shown in Figure 17-4.

3. Click OK when you are done.

> **NOTE** You can type multiple e-mails for a contact. To set one as the primary e-mail address, highlight it, and click Set Preferred.

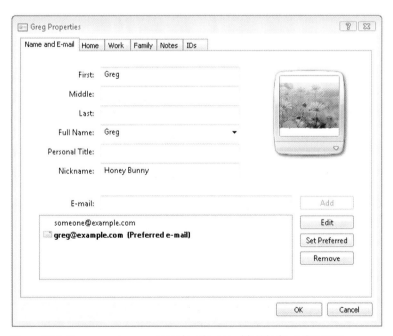

**Figure 17-4:** You can set up contacts in minutes with Windows Contacts.

Tired of someone on your contact list? Yeah, we get irritated with people too. Just right-click a contact in Windows Contacts, and click Delete. Poof! Gone from your life forever! Well, at least they are gone from your contacts list.

Take some time to play around in Windows Contacts. For instance, you can change the Contact view by clicking View in the menu and scrolling up and down. And you can create contact groups by clicking New Contact Group and selecting Add To Contact Group. It's so easy that we aren't even bothering with the steps here, people! Click and add, click and add...you can do this in your sleep (if you're an insomniac).

# Set Your RSS Options in Office Outlook 2007

In the previous chapter, we talked a bit about RSS feeds. These contain digital content frequently updated by Web sites, blogs, and other Internet locations. It's a great way for people to distribute information in a standard format, and you can read RSS feeds in a couple of ways. One is through Windows Internet Explorer 7 in Windows Vista (covered in the previous chapter); others are through Microsoft Office Outlook 2007 and the Windows Sidebar (through the addition of a gadget that contains the feed you want, as explained in Chapter 14).

Since we haven't covered RSS feeds in Outlook 2007 yet, we'll do that here. When you subscribe to a feed, a new folder is automatically created in your Mail folders called RSS Subscriptions. But before you can read a feed in Outlook 2007, you must add it to your account settings.

### ADD AN RSS FEED TO OUTLOOK 2007

5 minutes

To add an RSS feed to Outlook 2007, follow these steps:

1. Open Outlook 2007. Click Tools, and click Account Settings.

2. Click New on the RSS Feeds tab.

3. Type the location of the RSS feed you want to add. Click Add.

4. Click OK.

Now, refer to your mail folders for the RSS Subscriptions folder. It might take a few minutes to appear, but it will eventually be there, waiting for you with regular updates.

# Use Network Features

If networks make you nervous, the new Windows Vista Network and Sharing Center (shown in Figure 17-5) will ease your fears a bit. It was designed for people like you who don't typically think about networks but have more than one computer in

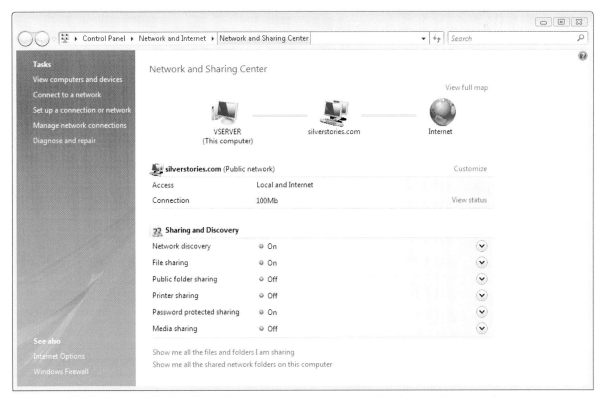

**Figure 17-5:** The Network and Sharing Center lets you see and troubleshoot network connections at a glance.

the home or office. Networks let you share files and hardware easily—you can add a single printer, for example, to a network for multiple people to use. Most people use networks in office settings, but they are becoming more common at home as Dad uses the laptop in the kitchen, Mom finishes some work in the basement, and the kids play games in the living room. Multiple computers might be a necessity for these various activities and locations, but multiple printers don't have to be!

A Network Setup Wizard helps you set up wired or wireless networks and then shows you with an illustrated map how your network is connected and where any problems are. Once you have your network set up, Windows Vista prevents you from connecting to fraudulent wireless networks, looks for changing capabilities (such as firewall settings that may change from home to office), and even adjusts to receive more data by detecting the speed of your Internet connection and the bandwidth available. The Network and Sharing Center exploration won't take much time for you at all, but if you waited until now to set up your network, be prepared to spend a couple of hours hooking everything up and following the steps involved.

### SET UP A NETWORK

 **2 to 3 hours**

We aren't going to explain step by step in this book how to set up a home or office network; the Windows Vista Network Wizard does that for you. We will assume you already know what you need for your network and have obtained the correct hardware for setting it up. If you're not sure, you can get help from your local computer store. When you are ready to set up a network, follow these steps:

1 Open the Network and Sharing Center (Start button, Start Search box).

2 Click Set Up A Connection Or Network in the Tasks pane.

3 Follow the wizard instructions for your particular installation.

Once the network is set up, you can access the additional Network and Sharing Center features via the Tasks pane:

**View Computers And Devices**  Lets you see all the computers and devices currently part of your network. This helps you confirm an item was added to your network and can be used to open a network resource, such as a printer or another computer.

**Connect To A Network**   Lets you connect to other computer networks.

**Manage Network Connections**   Takes you to a folder that stores all your network connections, such as for a network, the Internet, or a virtual private network.

**Diagnose And Repair**   Gives you access to automated diagnostics to help you troubleshoot problems within your network, such as connection problems.

Setting up a network is never going to be a piece of cake, but with the helpful wizard in Windows Vista, the task is much easier than ever before. Grab some snacks and caffeine, and get started—you'll love having a network if you have more than one computer in your life.

# Go on the Road with Remote Desktop Connection and Remote Assistance

Two different types of remote connections can help you get work done and seek real-time help when you need it.

## REMOTE DESKTOP CONNECTION

Why on Earth do you need a Remote Desktop Connection? If you have to ask, you've never used one. Boy, are *you* in for a treat! Remote Desktop Connections can save time and aggravation: It's a technology already installed in Windows Vista that lets you sit at a computer in one place and connect to another computer in a completely different physical location away from you. For example, you can leave programs running on your computer at work and then see them—the same way you do at work—when you turn on your computer at home. You can be miles away from the work computer but be working on it as if you had never left the office. The remote computer screen will appear blank to anyone at the remote location.

There are some prerequisites to connect to a remote computer:

- The remote computer must be turned on.

- The remote computer must have a network or Internet connection.

- The remote computer must have Remote Desktop turned on. (See the note regarding limitations.)

- You must have network access to the remote computer. (Internet connections are okay.)

- You must have permission to connect. (You must be on the list of users for the remote computer.)

**NOTE** You cannot use a Remote Desktop Connection to connect *to* computers running Vista Starter, Home Basic, Home Basic N, or Home Premium. You can only *create* a connection *from* those editions of Windows Vista. In addition, you can't use a Remote Desktop connection to connect to computers running Windows XP Home Edition.

## ALLOW REMOTE CONNECTIONS

 10 minutes

To allow remote connections on the computer you want to connect to, follow these steps:

1. On the computer you want to allow a connection to, open the system through the Control Panel. (Look under System and Maintenance, System.)

2. Click Remote Settings. Under Remote Desktop, select one of the two Allow Connections options. Click Help Me Choose if you're not sure which one is right for you. You may be prompted for an administrator password or confirmation during this step.

3. Click Select Users.

4. In the Remote Desktop Users dialog box, click Add to add your name.

5. In the Select Users dialog box, click Locations, and choose the location you want to search.

6. In the Enter The Object Names To Select box, type the name of the user to add. Click OK.

7. In the System Properties dialog box, click OK.

## START REMOTE DESKTOP

**5 minutes or less**

To start Remote Desktop on the computer you want to work from, follow these steps:

1. Open Remote Desktop Connection (click the Start button, and search for Remote Desktop Connection).

2. In Computer, type the name of the computer to which you will be connecting. You can type the IP address of the computer instead of the name if you prefer. If you don't know your computer's name, click the Start button, and then click Welcome Center. The computer name will be at the top of the window.

3. Click Connect.

## USE WINDOWS REMOTE ASSISTANCE

Remote connections are great because they can save you time and aggravation, especially when something you need is on a computer miles away. Another remote connection exists that we want to share with you. This one comes in handy when you're working on your computer and need help...or when someone you know needs help on their computer. It's called Windows Remote Assistance.

This program connects two computers so that one person can help another troubleshoot or fix computer problems in real time. Let's say you need help fixing a graphic in Microsoft Office PowerPoint 2007. You can connect to a buddy who is an expert at PowerPoint 2007, and they can see your screen and also can take over and actually fix the problem for you while you watch. When they're done, you get control of your computer back, and your problem is fixed. We use this particular feature with elderly parents, by the way. It's much easier to just let Mom ask for help and jump on her computer to fix the problem than to spend endless time explaining what the cursor should look like when it has properly grasped an object. You may have similar people in your life who need occasional help—or perhaps you're the one who needs help. Either way, using Remote Assistance can be an invaluable time-saver. A big difference between this and Remote Desktop Connection is that both parties can see the screen with Remote Assistance; just one location can see the screen with Remote Desktop Connection.

## GET HELP WITH WINDOWS REMOTE ASSISTANCE

 **2 minutes**

To get help with Windows Remote Assistance, follow these steps:

1. Open Windows Remote Assistance through the Start button and the Start Search box.

2. Click Invite Someone You Trust To Help You.

3. Click Use E-Mail To Send An Invitation (if you used Web-based e-mail, choose the other option).

4. Type a password of at least six characters. Click Next. Remote Assistance will open a new e-mail for you, as shown in Figure 17-6; this might take a minute or two if your e-mail program is not open.

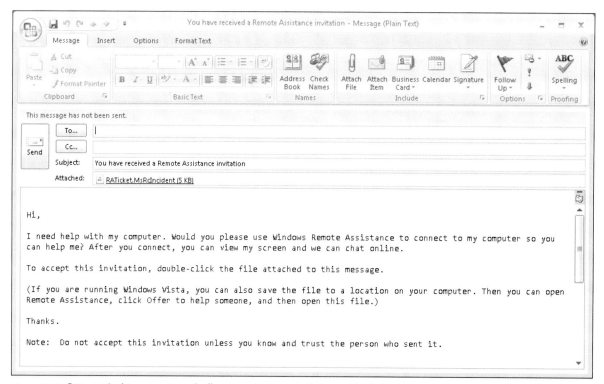

Figure 17-6: Remote Assistance automatically generates an e-mail request for help.

⑤ Type the e-mail address of the person you are sending the invitation to in the To line of the automatically generated e-mail that appears. Note that an attachment has been added to the e-mail; the recipient will open that attachment to access your computer.

⑥ Be sure to add the password to the e-mail. This will not be automatically generated for you.

⑦ Click Send.

⑧ When the other person accepts your request for help, you will be asked whether that person can connect to your computer. Click Yes.

**NOTE** You must remain connected to Remote Assistance while waiting for the other person to respond. If you disconnect before they respond, the invitation is no longer valid, and the other person will have to reenter the invitation file location.

⑨ When you are ready to disconnect from the session with your helper, click Disconnect in the Connected To Your Helper dialog box.

You can use three options with this program—Pause, Chat, and Send File. Chat is especially useful to explain to your helper what you need help with, unless you prefer chatting via phone. Your helper can also ask to take control of your computer (see Figure 17-7); a message will appear asking you for approval before control transfers over. Once control is given, you will see everything your helper does on your computer, but you will also be able to work on your screen. When you want to stop sharing control, just click Stop Sharing.

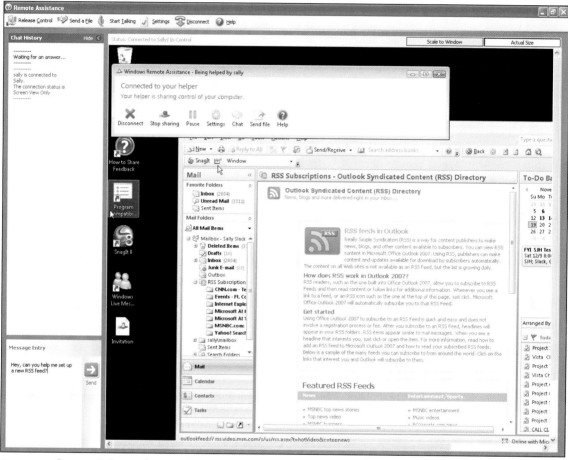

**Figure 17-7:** Remote Assistance lets another user in another location not only see your screen but perform tasks on your computer as well.

We wish we had more space so we could continue sharing with you all the great features in Windows Vista. In this chapter, we hit the highlights of Windows Mail, Windows Contacts, RSS feeds, the new Network and Sharing Center, Remote Desktop Connection, and Remote Assistance. Whew! Windows Vista tossed in a lot of extra stuff to help you out. Take the time to play around with these features, and don't be afraid to get your hands sweaty with fear. You can't really mess up much with Windows Vista, and if you do, Help isn't far. We've enjoyed sharing tips with you to help you jump in and get started quickly with all kinds of Windows Vista features and programs.

# Index

# About the Authors

**Joli Ballew** is a technical author, a technology trainer, and a media and media gadget enthusiast. Joli currently runs and manages several media setups, including running Windows Vista Ultimate to power a Media Center PC to record television and manage her media, using a Zune for portable music and video, using a wireless network with security cameras that record movement for home protection, connecting to a wired network with five PCs in a workgroup all with shared data, working with shared media on a second Media Center PC running Windows Vista Ultimate using Media Player 11, and running multiple wired and wireless streaming video and music scenarios.

Joli has several certifications including MCSE, A+, and MCDST, and has a bachelor's degree in mathematics. In addition to writing, she occasionally teaches computer classes at the local junior college (including one for teens on how to build their own computer) and works as a network administrator and Web designer for North Texas Graphics. She has written almost two dozen books, including *Degunking Windows* (Paraglyph Press), which was awarded the IPPY for best computer book of the year in 2005; *PC Magazine: Office 2007 Solutions* (Wiley); and the delightfully popular book *Microsoft Windows XP: Do Amazing Things!* (Microsoft Press). Joli also writes for Microsoft's Windows XP Expert Zone and the Vista Community Web site, writes and gives Microsoft Webcasts, and is an occasional Microsoft blogger. Joli has also written a textbook for Microsoft's MCDST certification. In her free time, she enjoys golfing, doing yard work, exercising at the local gym, and teaching her cat, Pico, tricks.

**Sally Slack** is a writer and author with more than 16 years of experience in business and technical writing. She specializes in demystifying complex topics so consumers can both understand and apply difficult concepts. Slack has written numerous articles for small- and medium-sized businesses, appearing internationally in business magazines and online business sites. She has also been an executive and business transformation communications consultant to IBM, Lenovo International, and State Farm Insurance Cos., and routinely writes for Microsoft, IBM, Sony, and other companies. She is a regular contributor to the Microsoft At Home, At Work, Vista Community, and Work Essentials Web sites. As a corporate consultant, she has written general, strategic, marketing, and technical internal communications and education material (including complete courses, case studies, brochures, training guides, tip sheets, and testing materials in both print and online formats).

Her other books include *PC Magazine: Office 2007 Solutions* (Wiley), *CNET Do-It-Yourself Digital Home Office Projects: 24 Cool Things You Didn't Know You Could Do!* (McGraw-Hill), *The Financial Advisor's Guide to the Microsoft Office System* (Agility Press), *The Accountant's and Auditor's Guide to the Microsoft Office System* (Agility Press), *The Financial Analyst's Guide to the Microsoft Office System* (Agility Press), and *A Public Relations Survival Kit* (Grendel Press).

In her free time, she enjoys spending time with her family, boating, traveling, and trying the latest high-tech gadgets and applications available. Her cats, Bugsy and Madeline, flatly refuse to learn tricks.

# What do you think of this book?

# We want to hear from you!

Do you have a few minutes to participate in a brief online survey?

Microsoft is interested in hearing your feedback so we can continually improve our books and learning resources for you.

To participate in our survey, please visit:

**www.microsoft.com/learning/booksurvey/**

...and enter this book's ISBN-10 number (appears above barcode on back cover*). As a thank-you to survey participants in the United States and Canada, each month we'll randomly select five respondents to win one of five $100 gift certificates from a leading online merchant. At the conclusion of the survey, you can enter the drawing by providing your e-mail address, which will be used for prize notification only.

Thanks in advance for your input. Your opinion counts!

\* Where to find the ISBN-10 on back cover

ISBN-13: 000-0-0000-00000-0
ISBN-10: 0-0000-00000

0 00000 00000    0 0000

0  000000 000000

Example only. Each book has unique ISBN.

*Microsoft* Press

**www.microsoft.com/learning/booksurvey/**